THE BEST OF
Wood Boxes

THE BEST OF
Wood Boxes

Edited by R. Adam Blake

POPULAR WOODWORKING BOOKS
CINCINNATI, OHIO

To prevent accidents, keep safety in mind while you work. Use the safety guards installed on power equipment, keep fingers away from saw blades, wear safety goggles to prevent injuries from flying wood chips and sawdust, wear headphones to protect your hearing, and consider installing a dust vacuum to reduce the amount of airborne sawdust in your woodshop. Don't wear loose clothing, such as neckties or shirts with loose sleeves, or jewelry, such as rings, necklaces or bracelets, when working on power equipment, and tie back long hair to prevent it from getting caught in your equipment. The author and editors who compiled this book have tried to make all the contents as accurate and correct as possible. Plans, illustrations, photographs and text have been carefully checked. All instructions, plans and projects should be carefully read, studied and understood before beginning construction. Due to the variability of local conditions, construction materials, skill levels, etc., neither the authors nor Popular Woodworking Books assumes any responsibility for any accidents, injuries, damages or other losses incurred resulting from the material presented in this book.

The Best of Wood Boxes. Copyright © 1998 by Popular Woodworking Books. Manufactured in China. All rights reserved. No part of this book may be reproduced in any form or by any electronic or mechanical means including information storage and retrieval systems without permission in writing from the publisher, except by a reviewer, who may quote brief passages in a review. Published by Popular Woodworking Books, an imprint of F&W Publications, Inc., 1507 Dana Avenue, Cincinnati, Ohio 45207. (800) 289-0963. First edition.

Other fine Popular Woodworking Books are available from your local bookstore or direct from the publisher.

All projects in this book are designed to be made in the home workshop. They are intended solely for personal use, not for commercial sale or manufacture.

02 01 00 99 98   5 4 3 2 1

Library of Congress Cataloging-in-Publication Data

The best of wood boxes / edited by R. Adam Blake.

p.   cm.
ISBN 1-55870-476-0 (alk. paper)
1. Wooden boxes. I. Blake, R. Adam.
NK9955.B6B47   1998
745.51—DC21   97-36422
                                       CIP

Edited by R. Adam Blake
Content Edited by Bruce E. Stoker
Production Edited by Michelle Kramer
Interior and cover designed by Angela Lennert Wilcox

METRIC CONVERSION CHART

TO CONVERT	TO	MULTIPLY BY
Inches	Centimeters	2.54
Centimeters	Inches	0.4
Feet	Centimeters	30.5
Centimeters	Feet	0.03
Yards	Meters	0.9
Meters	Yards	1.1
Sq. Inches	Sq. Centimeters	6.45
Sq. Centimeters	Sq. Inches	0.16
Sq. Feet	Sq. Meters	0.09
Sq. Meters	Sq. Feet	10.8
Sq. Yards	Sq. Meters	0.8
Sq. Meters	Sq. Yards	1.2
Pounds	Kilograms	0.45
Kilograms	Pounds	2.2
Ounces	Grams	28.4
Grams	Ounces	0.04

ABOUT THIS BOOK

Boxes are fascinating. Most of us slept in a sort of box as infants. As young children, many of us are told, we were often more interested in the boxes or containers than the gifts they were meant to conceal until opened. We used them as houses, forts and caves; cars, boats and spaceships; hats, shoes and armor. As we grow up, boxes become increasingly important. They hold important things we want to save; unimportant things we want to discard; and all the other stuff we don't quite know what to do with. Large boxes hold our clothes while traveling or hide our television sets when not in use. Smaller ones store our cigars, jewelry or mementos. And eventually, forgive me for being morbid, many of us will have to choose a large box for ourselves or a loved one in preparation for our physical death.

We took this idea about the box, that it has inherent appeal to just about everyone, and we created a book to showcase the work of some of the best box makers in the world. After a few months of soliciting submissions for the book, we sorted through nearly a hundred entries and chose the boxes featured in this book. These boxes are just a small sample of the hundreds of woodworkers who are making boxes, whether professionally or as amateurs, whether for sale or for gifts, whether for pure aesthetic reasons or for simple pragmatic ones.

This book is meant to be a "swipefile." That is, you, the reader, whether a novice or professional woodworker, should be able to pick up this book and find inspiration for creating and building your own boxes. Examine the photos, read the project descriptions and create your own designs. Remember, all of the designs in this book are legally copyrighted to the creators of each box (imitation may be the sincerest form of flattery, but it's also one of the quickest ways to meet a lawyer—or need one). So, let your own dreams inspire you, make your box bigger, make your box smaller, but whatever you do, make the box your own.

Who knows, maybe someday you'll find yourself in volume two.

TABLE OF CONTENTS

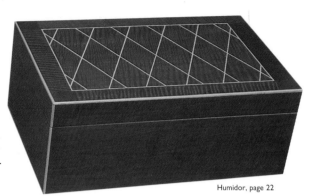

Humidor, page 22

Double CD Cabinet, page 34

The Empress Collection, page 92

Treasure Box, page 12

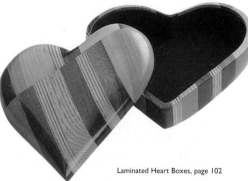

Laminated Heart Boxes, page 102

Turkish Lidded Box, page 54

Turned Lattice Box, page 14

Collector's Box, page 10

Retro Sleek, page 72

Leather/Ebony, page 98

Collector's Box With Drawer

WILLIAM A. GEORGE

NAME: William A. George
HOME: San Antonio, Texas
PROJECT: Collector's Box With Drawer
DIMENSIONS: 12″ × 7½″ × 4½″
MATERIALS: Pear, cherry, maple, Ebon-X, Madrone burl, mesquite
FINISH: Minwax Helmsman Urethane
TIME SPENT: 20 hours
MATERIALS COST: $25
RETAIL PRICE: $385

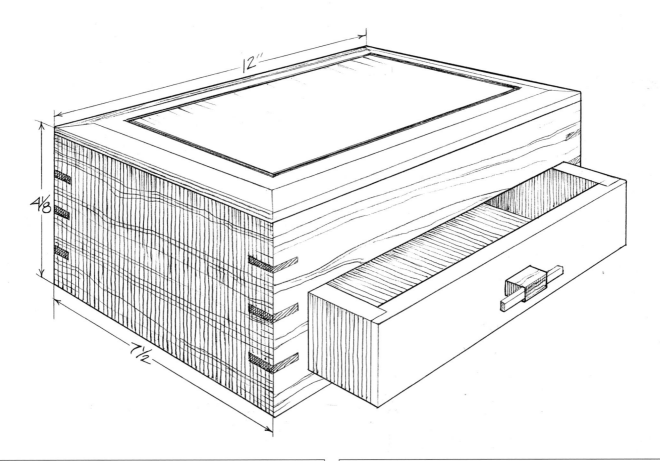

B ILL GEORGE is a lifelong woodworker who made craft items and furniture as a hobby. After a class in fine furniture construction, he designed this box as a test of several ideas of how to make a living making fine furniture and interior accents. Bill's goal in making this box was to make a fine, custom interior accent using shop scraps.

PROJECT DESCRIPTION

The joinery for this box is quite simple. The outer box sides are mitered and joined with biscuits. The inner box sides are rabbet joints, and the dividers are half laps or "egg crate" constructions. The mid bottom is captured in a groove in the sides, and the low bottom fits into rabbets cut into the edge of the box sides.

MATERIALS LIST

Box side (2) $\frac{5}{8}'' \times 3\frac{3}{4}'' \times 7\frac{1}{2}''$ pear
Box front/back (2) $\frac{5}{8}'' \times 3\frac{3}{4}'' \times 12''$ pear
Inner box side (2) $\frac{1}{4}'' \times 1'' \times 6\frac{3}{8}''$ maple
Inner box front/back (2) $\frac{1}{4}'' \times 1'' \times 10\frac{3}{4}''$ maple
Inner box long divider (2) $\frac{1}{4}'' \times \frac{3}{4}'' \times 10\frac{3}{8}''$ maple
Inner box short divider (3) $\frac{1}{8}'' \times \frac{1}{2}'' \times 6\frac{1}{8}''$ maple
Mid bottom (1) $\frac{1}{4}'' \times 6\frac{7}{8}'' \times 11\frac{3}{16}''$ MDF
Low bottom (1) $\frac{1}{8}'' \times 6\frac{7}{8}'' \times 11\frac{3}{16}''$ plywood
Drawer front (1) $\frac{1}{2}'' \times 1\frac{1}{2}'' \times 10''$ figured maple
Drawer back (1) $\frac{1}{4}'' \times 1\frac{1}{8}'' \times 10''$ maple
Drawer side (2) $\frac{1}{4}'' \times \frac{1}{2}'' \times 6\frac{13}{16}''$ maple
Drawer bottom (1) $\frac{1}{8}'' \times 9\frac{9}{16}'' \times 6\frac{11}{16}''$ plywood
Box in drawer, sides (2) $\frac{1}{8}'' \times \frac{3}{4}'' \times 6\frac{1}{4}''$ maple
Box in drawer, front/back (2) $\frac{1}{8}'' \times \frac{3}{4}'' \times 9\frac{5}{16}''$ maple
Lid frame sides (2) $\frac{5}{8}'' \times 1\frac{1}{4}'' \times 7\frac{1}{2}''$ cherry
Lid frame front/back (2) $\frac{5}{8}'' \times 1\frac{1}{4}'' \times 12''$ cherry
Lid panel (1) $\frac{1}{4}'' \times 5\frac{1}{2}'' \times 10\frac{7}{8}''$ MDF
Drawer slides (2) $\frac{3}{4}'' \times 2'' \times 6\frac{3}{8}''$ maple
Trim for lid (1) $\frac{1}{8}'' \times \frac{1}{8}'' \times 36''$ Ebon-X
Trim for bottom (1) $\frac{1}{8}'' \times \frac{1}{8}'' \times 36''$ maple
Maple veneer for lid bottom
Madrone burl veneer for lid top

Treasured Box

DEWEY GARRETT

NAME: Dewey Garrett
HOME: Livermore, California
PROJECT: Treasured Box
DIMENSIONS: 8″ diameter × 4″ high
MATERIALS: Ebony, pink ivory
FINISH: Wax
TIME SPENT: 40 hours
MATERIALS COST: $40
RETAIL PRICE: $650

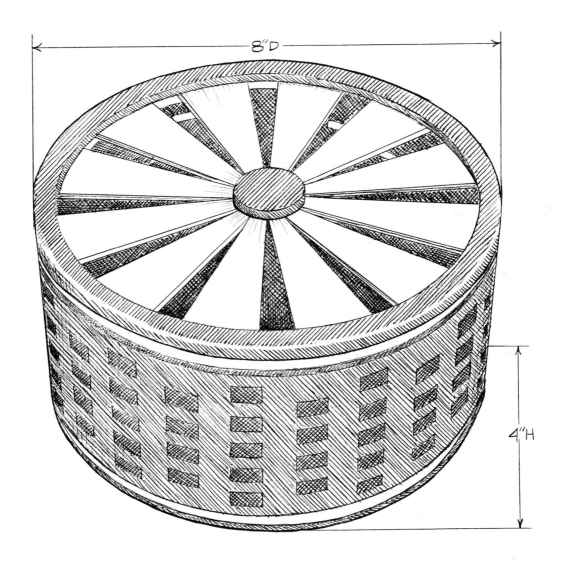

8″D

4″H

I wanted to make a fairly large box that used precious materials—ebony and ivory—with very little waste." This design supports the goal and wastes very little material. ～

PROJECT DESCRIPTION

The box and lid are built up and turned one layer at a time. The lid is carefully fitted to the box.

MATERIALS LIST

(4-5) 1″ × 1″ × 12″ ebony
(4-5) 1″ × 1″ × 6″ ivory

Turned Lattice Box

DEWEY GARRETT

NAME: Dewey Garrett
HOME: Livermore, California
PROJECT: Turned Lattice Box
DIMENSIONS: 12″
  diameter × 4½″ high
MATERIALS: Cherry
FINISH: Deft Lacquer
TIME SPENT: 30 hours
MATERIALS COST: $10
RETAIL PRICE: $500

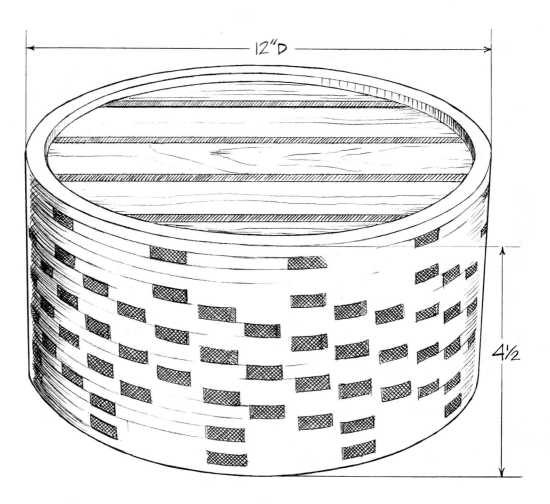

DEWEY GARRETT found wood turning so stimulating and challenging that it has become a 12-year, dedicated creative pursuit that complements his technical career. He is self-taught, and makes and modifies his tools to craft unique turnings. His work is a continuing exploration of the structure of forms constrained by the symmetry and simplicity imparted by the mechanics of a lathe. He is currently working on designs and methods that expose and combine turned shapes into new and unexpected compositions.

"I am always looking for ways to incorporate small scraps of wood and leftover pieces into my turnings. After making a large project in cherry, I had lots of ¼″ thick scraps and wanted to make a box."

PROJECT DESCRIPTION

There are two basic setups for this box: one for the lid and one for the box itself. The box is created one layer at a time by gluing up the ¼″ pieces to the previous layer and turning to shape, then repeat. There are 24 segments in each layer. The lid has a similar construction to a floating panel, except that it is of numerous pieces that are glued into the lid (see the detail inset drawing).

MATERIALS LIST

About two board feet of cherry scrap planed to ¼″ thick; random lengths.

Deco Chest

JIM FIOLA

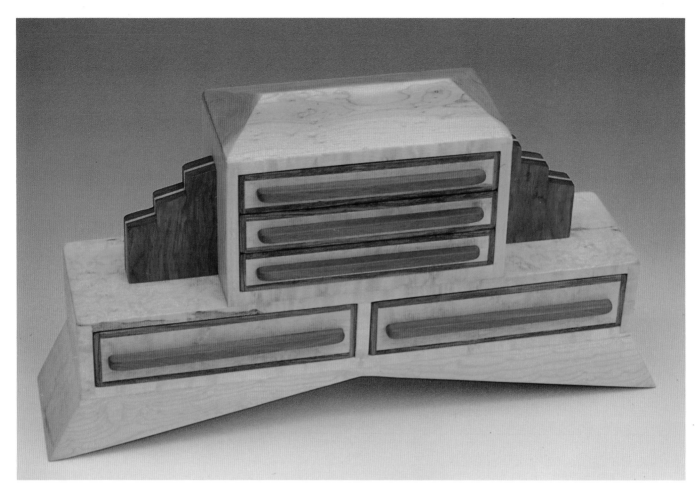

NAME: Jim Fiola

HOME: Branchville, New Jersey

PROJECT: Deco Chest

DIMENSIONS: 5½″ × 12″ × 22″

MATERIALS: Bird's-eye maple, bubinga

FINISH: Hand-dipped Watco, steel wool finish with linseed oil

TIME SPENT: 10-12 hours

MATERIALS COST: $20-$25

RETAIL PRICE: $325

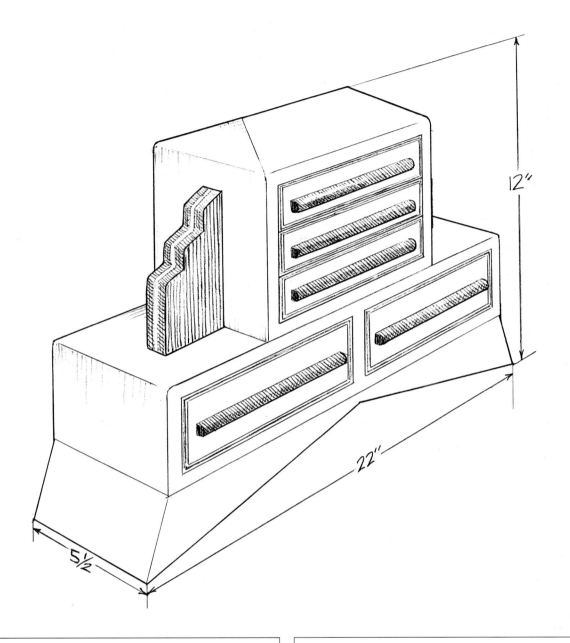

J IM FIOLA has been making boxes for more than 20
years. The "Deco Chest" comes from his desire to create
a piece that balances form with function in an Art Deco
flavor. "Function and form are very important to me. At
times the form of a design reduces the function. A fine balance has to be utilized to make any piece work." ⤳

PROJECT DESCRIPTION

The joinery for this box is quite simple; most, if not all, are
rabbet and dado joints. Perhaps the most difficult step is
cutting the 30°-35° angle for the crown piece.

MATERIALS LIST

Base front/back (2) ½" × 2½" × 22"
Base sides (2) ½" × 2½" × 4½"
Lower drawer section top/bottom (2) ½" × 5½" × 20"
Lower drawer section sides (2) ½" × 2¾" × 5½"
Lower drawer section middle divider (1) ½" × 2¼" × 5¼"
Lower drawers, outside dimensions (2) 5⅛" × 9¼" × 2¼"
Upper drawer section top/bottom (2) ½" × 5½" × 10"
Upper drawer section sides (2) ½" × 5¾" × 5½"
Upper drawers, outside dimensions (3) 1½" × 8⅞" × 5⅛"
Steps (2 each length) ¾" × 1" stock cut at 20° on upper end
    at 2⅝", 3⅜" and 4½"
Crown (1) 1" × 10" × 5½"

Hanging Recipe File Box

NORMAN CROWFOOT

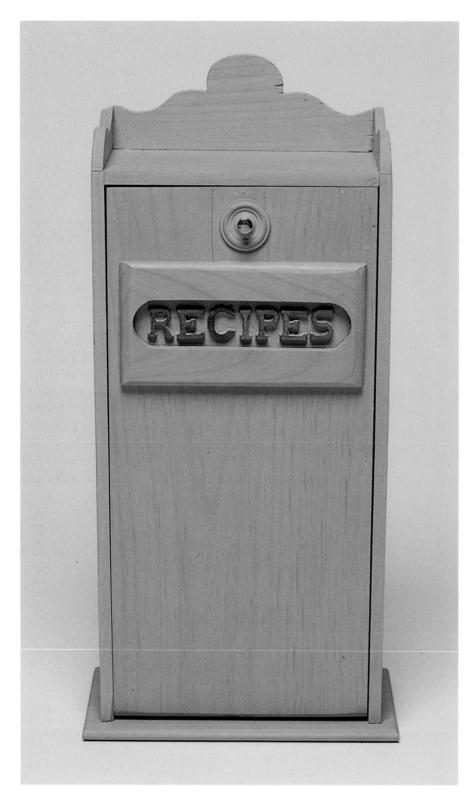

NAME: Norman Crowfoot
HOME: Tucson, Arizona
PROJECT: Hanging Recipe File Box
DIMENSIONS: 6¾″ × 14″ × 4¼″
MATERIALS: Walnut, birch or alder
FINISH: Oil or gel stain and lacquer sealer
TIME SPENT: 4 hours
MATERIALS COST: $17
RETAIL PRICE: $88

6¾"   4¼"

14"

RECIPES

NORMAN CROWFOOT (with the help of his friend Bob Bauer, Lakeside, Arizona) designed this box to save a lot of kitchen counter space used up by cookbooks. With the three sections, you can store more than 800 3″ × 5″ index cards. This box is designed to hang on the wall.

PROJECT DESCRIPTION

All the joints of this box are butt joints. The toughest part of the project is figuring out where to put the dowel pivot point. Once this is determined, the box will stay closed because of the cantilever action created by proper pivot point location. The top end of the drawer sides will need to be shortened, and the top drawer end will have to be angled to allow for clearance. The internal cleat is attached to the back so that the box front/file drawer bottom will stop in a horizontal position when the drawer is opened fully.

MATERIALS LIST

Box sides (2) ¼″ × 4¼″ × 12¾″
Box back (1) ¼″ × 6¾″ × 13¾″
Box bottom (1) ¼″ × 4⅛″ × 7¼″
Box top (1) ¼″ × 4″ × 6¼″
Box front/file drawer bottom (1)
¼″ × 6⅛″ × 13¾″
File drawer ends (2) ¼″ × 3¾″ × 5¾″
File drawer sides (2)
¼″ × 3¾″ × 11⅝″
Drawer dividers (2) ¼″ × 3¾″ × 5¾″
Internal cleat (1) ¼″ × ½″ × 6¼″

Humidor on a Stand

RICK ALLYN

NAME: Rick Allyn
HOME: Twin Falls, Idaho
PROJECT: Humidor on a Stand
DIMENSIONS: 16″ × 6″ × 9″; stand is 26″ tall
MATERIALS: Spanish cedar, veneer:
     carpathian elm burl, makore, holly,
     mahogany, rosewood; stand is walnut
FINISH: Shellac sealer, lacquer
TIME SPENT: 60 hours
MATERIALS COST: $180
RETAIL PRICE: $1,100

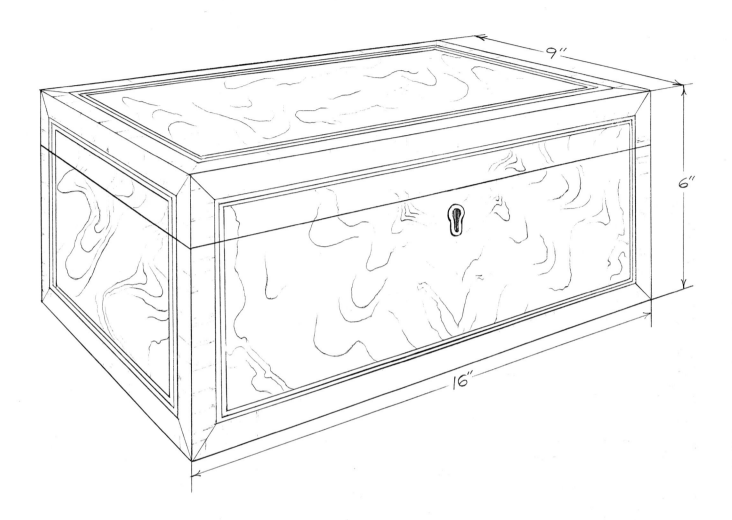

9"

6"

16"

RICK ALLYN was a self-taught woodworker until he enrolled in the fine woodworking program at the College of the Redwoods for one year. Although a professional furniture maker for 12 years, his 1993 move from San Diego to Idaho showed Allyn a tough furniture market, so he began to add humidors to his line. This humidor began as a spec job. Since it is "intentionally masculine," it is perhaps too large for most desks, hence the stand.

PROJECT DESCRIPTION

The humidor is primarily a plywood box (¼" top and ½" bottom) fitted with ¹⁄₁₆" spanish cedar and beautifully veneered. For the most part, the box is constructed with rabbet joints.

Humidor

RICK ALLYN

NAME: Rick Allyn

HOME: Twin Falls, Idaho

PROJECT: Humidor

DIMENSIONS: 12″ × 7″ × 5½″

MATERIALS: Spanish cedar, Makore veneer, holly inlay

FINISH: Lacquer

TIME SPENT: 25 hours

MATERIALS COST: $60

RETAIL PRICE: $495

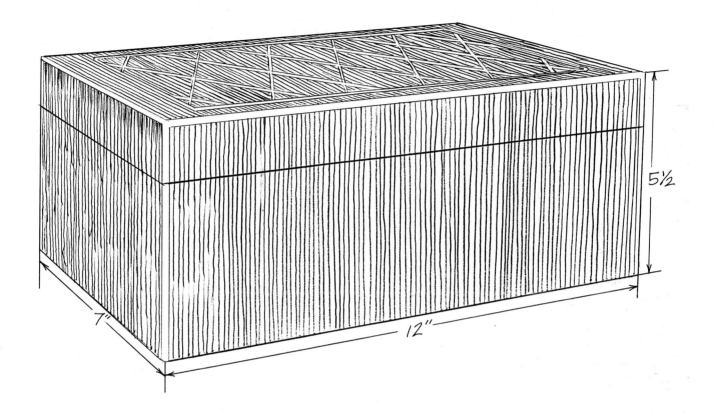

5½

7"

12"

T his is a smaller version of the previous humidor; it holds about 50 cigars. ◝

Dovetailed Box

RICK ALLYN

NAME: Rick Allyn

HOME: Twin Falls, Idaho

PROJECT: Dovetailed Box

DIMENSIONS: 10″ × 5″ × 3¾″

MATERIALS: Black acacia, spalted maple,
   Port Oxford cedar

FINISH: Shellac, wax

TIME SPENT: 8 hours

MATERIALS COST: $30

RETAIL PRICE: $170

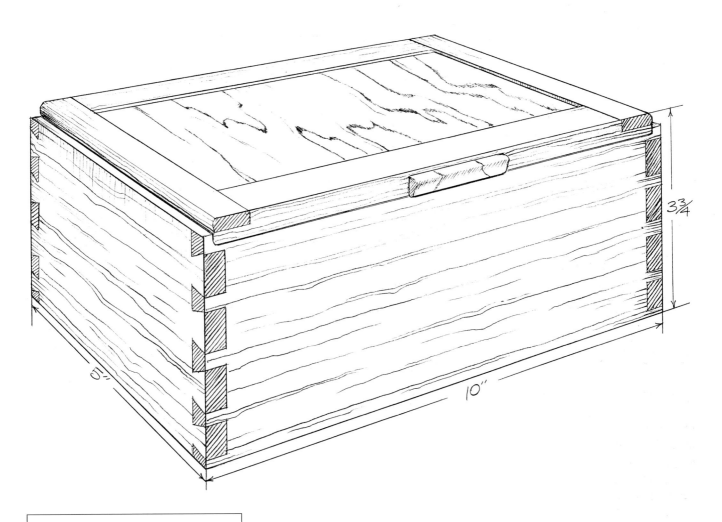

3¾

5″

10″

PROJECT DESCRIPTION

This box is inspired by a similar box
that Allyn learned to make at the
College of the Redwoods from James
Krenov.

Jewelry Box
RICK ALLYN

NAME: Rick Allyn
HOME: Twin Falls, Idaho
PROJECT: Jewelry Box
DIMENSIONS: 12″ × 7″ × 5″
MATERIALS: Bird's-eye maple, dyed curly
maple, rosewood
FINISH: Lacquer
TIME SPENT: 15 hours
MATERIALS COST: $60
RETAIL PRICE: $270

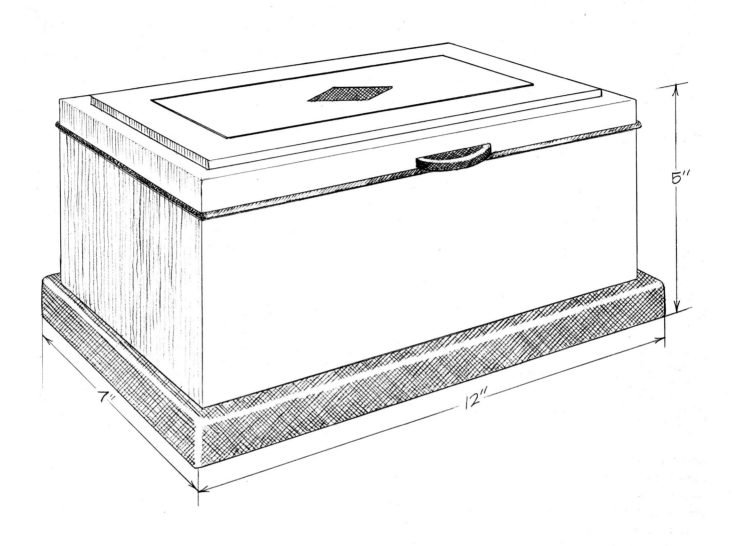

5"

7"

12"

Coopered Top Box

RICK ALLYN

NAME: Rick Allyn
HOME: Twin Falls, Idaho
PROJECT: Coopered Top Box
DIMENSIONS: 13″×9″×6″
MATERIALS: Alder
FINISH: Shellac
TIME SPENT: 18 hours
MATERIALS COST: $22
RETAIL PRICE: $325

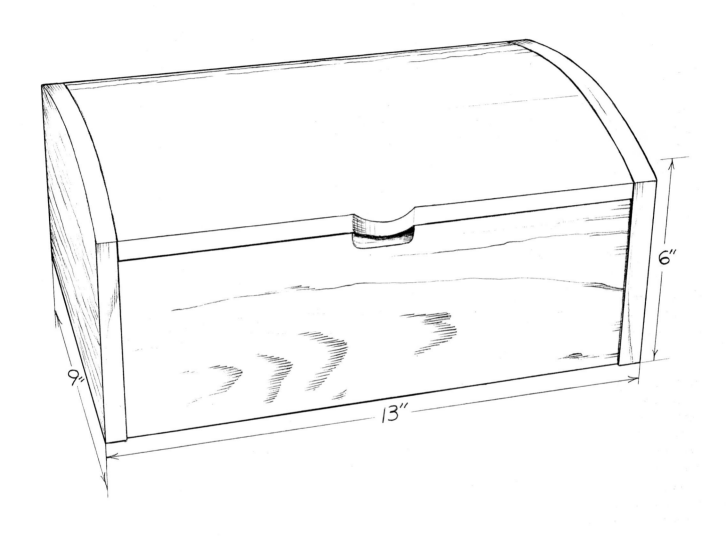

9"

13"

6"

Silverware Box
RICK ALLYN

NAME: Rick Allyn

HOME: Twin Falls, Idaho

PROJECT: Silverware Box

DIMENSIONS: 18″ × 20″ × 5″

MATERIALS: Curly maple, cedar

FINISH: Bartley's Gel Varnish

TIME SPENT: 8 hours

MATERIALS COST: $35

RETAIL PRICE: $220

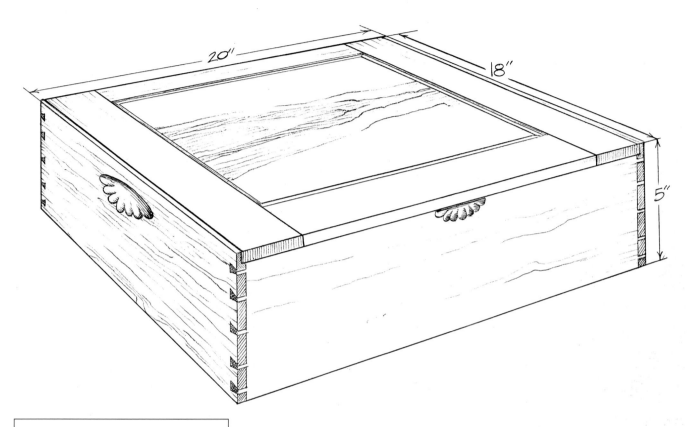

A nother of Rick Allyn's customers needed a box that would
contain an anti-tarnish insert to hold
her silverware. 🌿

Single CD Cabinet

McADAMS DESIGN

This is the single-column version of the double CD cabinet. The images in both represent fanciful worlds with strong references to the Japanese design aesthetic, but employ elements as diverse as Japanese prints, Art Nouveau, Art Deco, the Pre-Raphaelites and William Morris.

MATERIALS LIST

Top/bottom (2) ½″ × 7″ × 7″
Left side (1) ½″ × 6″ × 16½″
Right side (1) ½″ × 6⅛″ × 16½″
Back (1) ¼″ × 5¾″ × 16½″ plywood
Door stiles (2) ½″ × 1¼″ × 16¼″
Door rails (2) ½″ × 1¼″ × 6½″
Door panel (1) ¼″ × 4½″ × 15″ plywood

PROJECT DESCRIPTION

The sides of the box are blind rabbeted into the top and bottom pieces. The door pivots on pins set into the top and bottom pieces. The cabinet is sized to accommodate two sets of plastic CD holders attached with double-sided tape. A ⁵⁄₁₆″ diameter magnet in the right side wall, 2″ from the bottom, holds the door closed.

NAME: McAdams Design (Joyce McAdams and David Robinson)
HOME: Fairhope, Alabama
PROJECT: Single CD Cabinet
DIMENSIONS: 7″ × 7″ × 20″
MATERIALS: Bird's-eye maple, cherry
FINISH: Minwax wipe-on satin polyurethane
TIME SPENT: 3 hours
MATERIALS COST: $15
RETAIL PRICE: $150

Double CD Cabinet

McADAMS DESIGN

NAME: McAdams Design (Joyce McAdams and David Robinson)

HOME: Fairhope, Alabama

PROJECT: Double CD Cabinet

DIMENSIONS: 7½″ × 13″ × 20″

MATERIALS: Maple

FINISH: Minwax wipe-on polyvarnish

TIME SPENT: 4 hours

MATERIALS COST: $25

RETAIL PRICE: $325

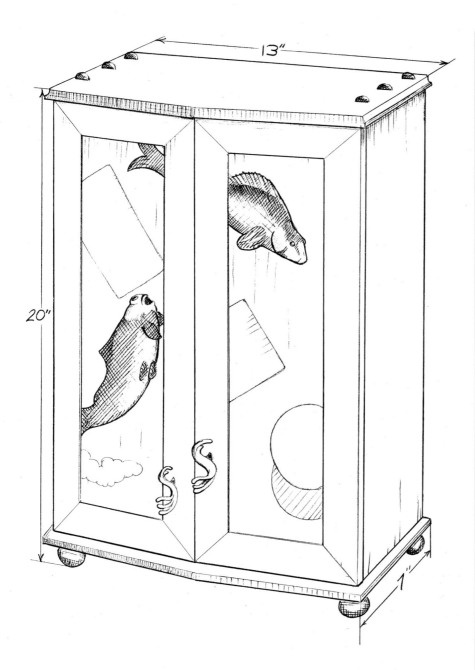

McADAMS DESIGN is the collaborative effort of husband-and-wife team Joyce McAdams and David Robinson. Their work strives to bring the complexity of ideas associated with the fine arts to functional objects, marrying fine hardwoods, craftsmanship and classic design with provocative images. The CD cabinet is one of a series of several related limited-production home accessories that are designed from an appreciation of the Arts and Crafts Movement, Japanese Mingei furniture and "a bit of post-modernism." ～

MATERIALS LIST

Top/bottom (2) ¾″ × 7½″ × 13″
Sides (2) ½″ × 6″ × 16½″
Mid rib (1) ¾″ × 6½″ × 16½″
Back (1) ¼″ × 11½″ × 16½″ plywood
Door stiles (4) ½″ × 1¼″ × 16½″
Door rails (4) ½″ × 1¼″ × 6¼″
Door panels (2) ¼″ × 4″ × 15½″ plywood

PROJECT DESCRIPTION

The joinery for this box is quite simple: mostly rabbet joints. After the top and bottom are cut to size and shape, a router is used to mill the profile to accept the sides and center panel. The doors are hinged with pins at the top and bottom. The doors are secured with ¼″ bullet catches at the bottom. The panels of these floating panel doors are dyed on the inside to match the accent buttons and ball feet, and to accent the image.

Ceremony Box

McADAMS DESIGN

NAME: McAdams Design (Joyce McAdams
    and David Robinson)
HOME: Fairhope, Alabama
PROJECT: Ceremony Box
DIMENSIONS: 10″ × 10″ × 3″
MATERIALS: Have used many varieties:
    maple, cherry, walnut, exotics
FINISH: Minwax Wipe-on polyurethane
TIME SPENT: 2½ hours
MATERIALS COST: $7
RETAIL PRICE: $135

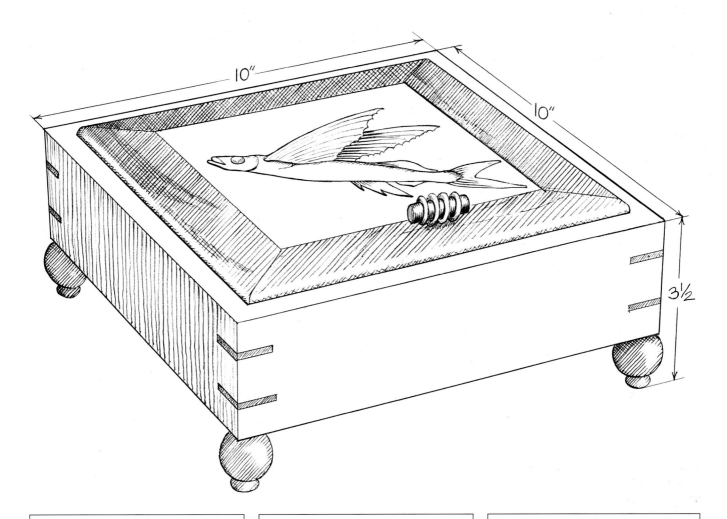

10"

10"

3½

This box is part of the series of home accessories inspired by the Arts and Crafts Movement, Japanese Mingei furniture and post-modernism.

PROJECT DESCRIPTION

This box is cut from ½" stock that is mitered and splined. The splines are chosen to accent the contrasting lid. The panel of this floating panel lid is dyed on the inside to match the accent buttons and ball feet, and to accent the image. The lid is hinged with pins through each side.

MATERIALS LIST

Sides (4) ½" × 10" × 2½"
Bottom (1) ⅛" × 9" × 9" plywood
Lid sides (4) ½" × 1¼" × 8½"
Lid top (1) ⅛" × 6½" × 6½" plywood

Poem Box
McADAMS DESIGN

NAME: McAdams Design (Joyce McAdams and David Robinson)

HOME: Fairhope, Alabama

PROJECT: Poem Box

DIMENSIONS: 7″ × 7½″ × 2½″

MATERIALS: Have used a wide variety: walnut, mahogany, maple, cherry, exotics

FINISH: Minwax Wipe-on polyurethane

TIME SPENT: 2 hours

MATERIALS COST: $5

RETAIL PRICE: $85

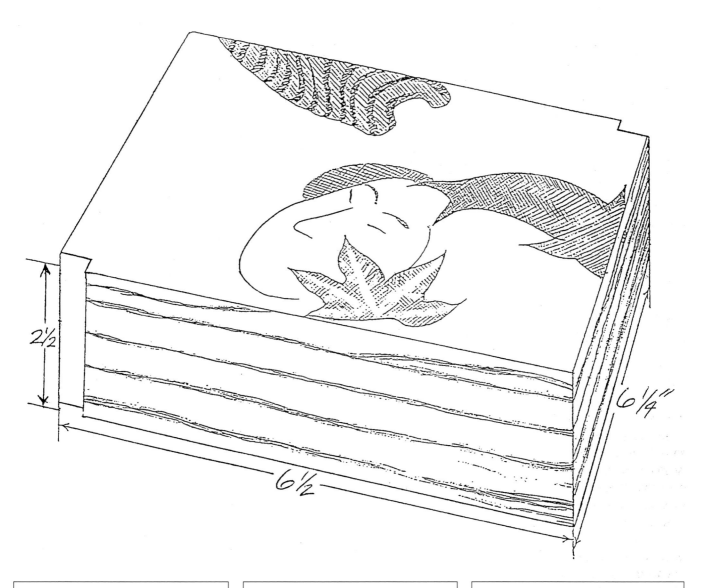

2½

6½

6¼"

This box was inspired by the 18th century Japanese boxes called Shikishi-boku, or "box for poems." They were plain lacquer boxes with an elaborate image on the lid used to store poems on square sheets of paper called Shikishi. They were designed to suggest overlapping sheets of paper. This redesign uses hardwood in place of lacquer and a one-of-a-kind image of acrylic artists paint, hand-dyed papers, and gold and silver leaf.

PROJECT DESCRIPTION

Two of the sides are mitered on one end and rabbeted on the other. The other two sides are mitered on one end. When assembled, they form the off-set design. The bottom is a floating panel. The top is let into the sides. After gluing and splining, the box is cut on a table saw to free the lid. The lid pivots on a dowel at the top right corner.

MATERIALS LIST

Top/bottom (2) ⅛″ × 5½″ × 5¾″ plywood
Side A (2) ¾″ × 2½″ × 6¼″
Side B (2) ¾″ × 2½″ × 6½″

Calligraphy and File Boxes

ROBERT SVERDUK

NAME: Robert Sverduk

HOME: Lake Ariel, Pennsylvania

PROJECT: Calligraphy box (top) and File box (bottom)

DIMENSIONS: Calligraphy box—10″ × 12½″ × 3″; file box—3½″ × 5½″ × 5″

MATERIALS: Calligraphy box—wild black cherry; file box—American walnut

3"

10"

12½

"Like Ben Franklin," says Robert Sverduk, " 'I do not remember when I could not read' and did not love reading." A long list of good authors has contributed greatly to a high appreciation for well-made tools and machinery and the beautiful objects that come from their skilled use. One very important reason for choosing to make fine boxes is that they are useful to just about everyone. The inspiration came from the development, by Sverduk, of the alignment machine that makes very fine, accurate dovetails. ~

PROJECT DESCRIPTION

The fine dovetails of these boxes were made with a machine built by Sverduk, as were the grooves for the dust seal lid. The hinges (inspired by a very old cork wine box acquired at a local "Country Auction") are made of strong fabric hidden by thin strips of matching wood. The calligraphy box, created by Sverduk for the Enslins, is large enough to hold standard letter-size paper and tabbed dividers and to allow the user to get their fingers in alongside the enclosed papers. The file box is large enough to accommodate stardard 3" × 5" file cards.

Marquetry Jewelry Box

BRETT HESSER

NAME: Brett Hesser

HOME: San Diego, California

PROJECT: Marquetry Jewelry Box

DIMENSIONS: 14″ × 14″ × 6″

MATERIALS: Curly maple, bubinga, walnut

FINISH: Oil/varnish mix

TIME SPENT: 100 hours

MATERIALS COST: $150

RETAIL PRICE: $2,650

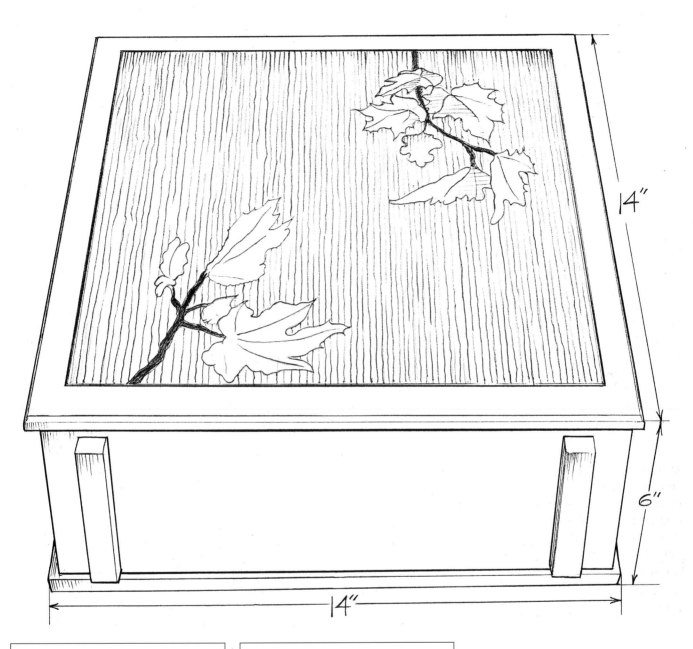

14"

6"

14"

B RETT HESSER learned marquetry from Silas Kopf at the
Leeds Design Workshop. This box
showcases the skills he learned. It
combines his love of Art Deco and
oriental forms with his woodworking
skills.

MATERIALS LIST

Sides (4) 14″×14″×6″
Drawer, outside dimensions (1)
    13″×13″×5½″

Inlaid Jewelry Box

BRETT HESSER

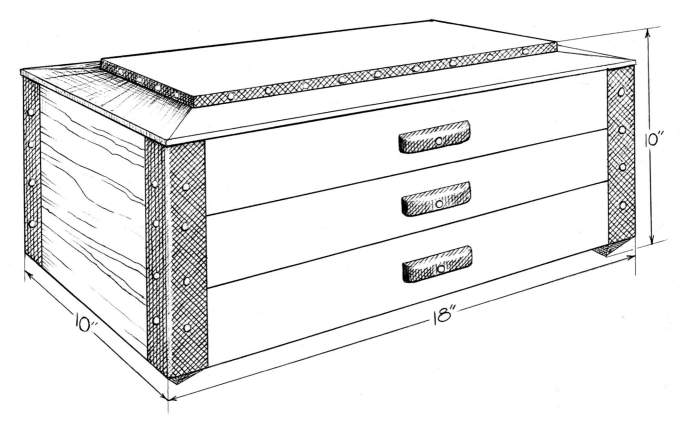

NAME: Brett Hesser
HOME: San Diego, California
PROJECT: Inlaid Jewelry Box
DIMENSIONS: 18″ × 10″ × 10″
MATERIALS: Honduran mahogany, ebony, ivory reclaimed from piano keys
FINISH: Conversion varnish
TIME SPENT: 75 hours
MATERIALS COST: $225
RETAIL PRICE: $2,700

BRETT HESSER developed his box-making skills while attending the Leeds Design Workshops. He enjoys box making because of the low budgets in materials and labor costs, as well as the ability to craft nice, small, shippable pieces with intricate detail. The inspiration for this box came from finding a turn-of-the-century piano that had fallen into extreme disrepair. The keys were made from ivory and ebony. Hesser wanted to show his ability to inlay these unique materials into wood. ～

MATERIALS LIST

Box top (1) 7¼″ × 7½″
Box back (1) 7¼″ × 15½″
Box sides (2) 7¼″ × 7½″
Drawer fronts (3) 15½″ × 3″

Moon Box

PATRICK LEONARD

NAME: Patrick Leonard

HOME: Washington, Pennsylvania

PROJECT: Moon Box

DIMENSIONS: 14″ × 13½″ × 7″

MATERIALS: Black walnut, bird's-eye maple

FINISH: Danish oil

TIME SPENT: 38 hours

MATERIALS COST: $75

RETAIL PRICE: $295

PATRICK LEONARD is a furniture builder by trade, but he has recently scaled down his pieces to small boxes. This allows his customers to have the artform, even if they have space restrictions. Inspired by the wood's characteristics, Leonard felt that both the crater-like appearance of the bird's-eye maple and the dark color of the walnut would imitate the ominous feeling of a full moon piercing the night sky.

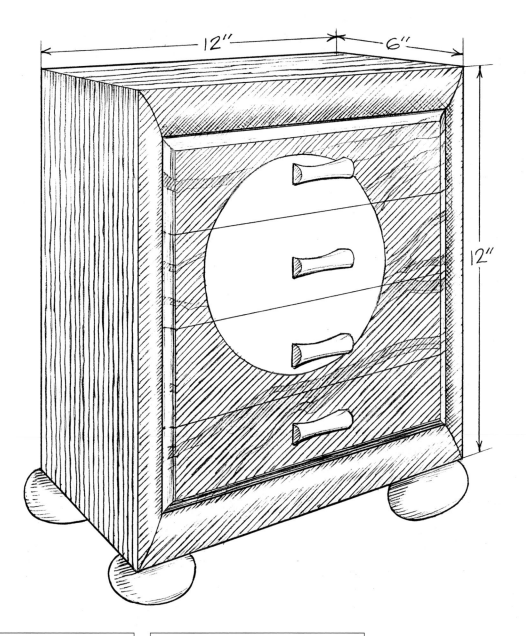

PROJECT DESCRIPTION

The "moon" on the face of the box is ⅛" bird's-eye maple inlaid into the walnut. The feet are turned, and the drawers ride on ½" invisible tracks.

MATERIALS LIST

Sides (4) ¾" × 6" × 12"
Drawer fronts (4) ½" × 2⁷⁄₁₆" × 10⁷⁄₁₆"
Drawer sides (8) ⅜" × 2⁷⁄₁₆" × 5½"
Drawer backs (4) ⅜" × 2⁷⁄₁₆" × 10¹⁄₁₆"
Drawer bottoms (4)
    ¼" × 5¼" × 10¹⁄₁₆"
Feet (4) 1" × 2¾" diameter

Mask Box

PO SHUN LEONG

NAME: Po Shun Leong

HOME: Winnetka, California

PROJECT: Mask Box

DIMENSIONS: 30" high

MATERIALS: Maple, koa, cherry, wenge, pernambuco, mahogany, buckeye burl, ebony

FINISH: Waterbased lacquer

TIME SPENT: 1 month

MATERIALS COST: $100

RETAIL PRICE: $9,000

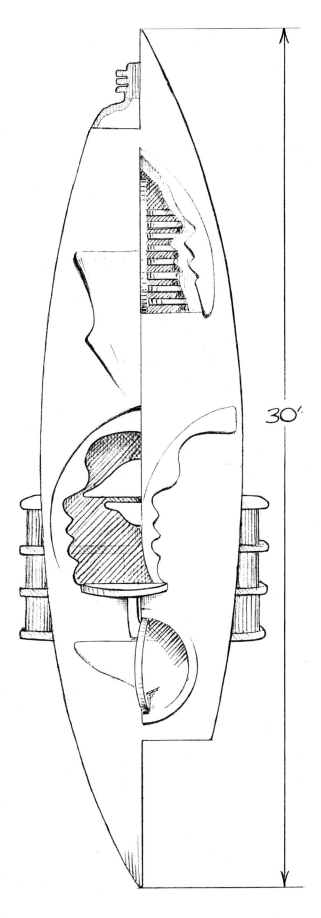

30"

Landscape Box
PO SHUN LEONG

NAME: Po Shun Leong

HOME: Winnetka, California

PROJECT: Landscape Box

DIMENSIONS: 20″ high

MATERIALS: Maple, koa, cherry, wenge, pernambuco, mahogany, buckeye burl, ebony

FINISH: Waterbased lacquer

TIME SPENT: 1 month

MATERIALS COST: $100

RETAIL PRICE: $5,900

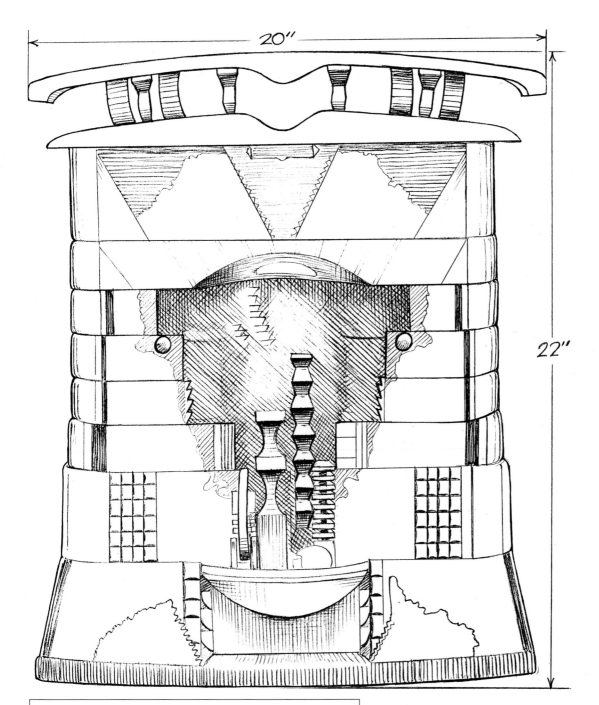

20"

22"

Self-taught woodworker Po Shun Leong is a former architect and furniture designer who makes sculptural containers that are visually dramatic. They are also strongly architectural in design. His boxes are exhibited in galleries and museums across the nation; in fact, a box similar to the "Landscape Box" shown in this book is on display in the White House Craft Collection. His carvings are inspired from legendary places of the past, present and future.

"It is up to the eye of the beholder to decide which place it is."

Tall Box
PO SHUN LEONG

NAME: Po Shun Leong
HOME: Winnetka, California
PROJECT: Tall Box
DIMENSIONS: 72″ high
MATERIALS: Maple, koa, cherry, wenge, pernambuco, mahogany, buckeye burl, ebony
FINISH: Waterbased lacquer
TIME SPENT: 1 month
MATERIALS COST: $100
RETAIL PRICE: $10,000

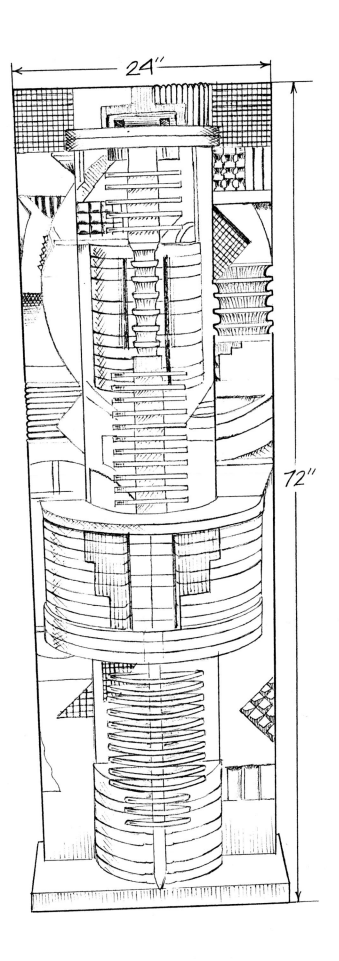

24"

72"

Many of Po Shun Leong's boxes are not planned on paper. In fact, most are conceptual sketches with rough outline dimensions. Details and materials are filled in as the box is created. The entire process is spontaneous.

Turkish Lidded Box

PETER LOWE

NAME: Peter Lowe
HOME: Floreat, Western Australia
PROJECT: Turkish Lidded Box
DIMENSIONS: 5⁵/₃₂″ × 4¼″ diameter
MATERIALS: Jarrah (Eucalyptus marginata)
FINISH: Lacquer
TIME SPENT: 1½ hours
MATERIALS COST: AUS $2
RETAIL PRICE: AUS $112.50

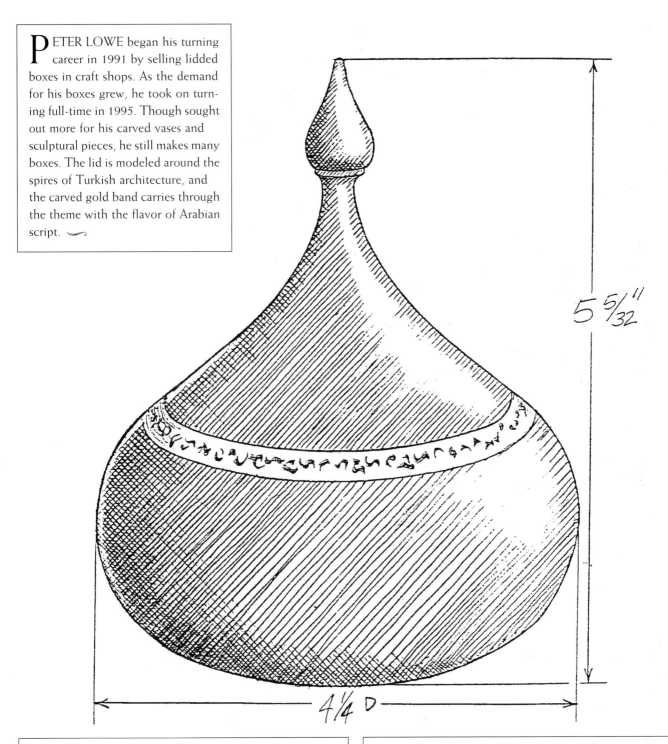

P ETER LOWE began his turning career in 1991 by selling lidded boxes in craft shops. As the demand for his boxes grew, he took on turning full-time in 1995. Though sought out more for his carved vases and sculptural pieces, he still makes many boxes. The lid is modeled around the spires of Turkish architecture, and the carved gold band carries through the theme with the flavor of Arabian script. ⌒

5 5/32"

4 1/4 D

PROJECT DESCRIPTION

The turning blocks are roughed to oversize about 3 months prior to final turning (be sure to use well-seasoned, stable stock). The rim of the lid is painted using gold spray paint from a can (overspray is turned away when dry). The gold band is then carved through to the base wood with a Dremel carver.

MATERIALS LIST

4⅜" × 4⅜" × 6" Jarrah (Eucalyptus marginata)

Nordic Boxes

LANCE LYERLY

NAME: Lance Lyerly
HOME: Floyd, Virginia
PROJECT: Nordic Boxes
DIMENSIONS: 10″ × 10″ × 12″
MATERIALS: Oak, cherry, walnut
FINISH: Linseed oil
TIME SPENT: 6-8 hours
MATERIALS COST: $12-$15
RETAIL PRICE: $80-$120

12"

10"

L ANCE LYERLY works in a custom church furniture shop. His
personal woodworking has him
"making a whole lot of weird things."
His enjoyment of Shaker boxes led
him to the similar Norwegian-style
oval boxes, which feature "ears" that
hold the lid on. Lyerly modified the
traditional design to incorporate a
dragon head for the latches. "I tell
people my boxes are Viking lunch
boxes. Everybody knows the Viking
reputation; they couldn't sail off to
battle carrying a Peter Pan lunch box,
now could they?" ⌐⌐

PROJECT DESCRIPTION

The box's body is steam bent and
fastened with copper nails. All you
really need to make this box is a band
saw, router and sander (and a
hammer and anvil to set the nails).
The most difficult part is getting the
latch just right: too tight, and the lid
won't come off; too loose, and the lid
will come off when you try to carry
it by the handle.

MATERIALS LIST

Box body (1) ⅛" × 6" × 36"
Lid (1) ¾" × 12" × 16"
Heads and handle (1) ¾" × 6" × 16"
Bottom (1) ¾" × 12" × 12"

Lap Desk

HENRY R. JEX

NAME: Henry R. Jex
HOME: Santa Monica, California
PROJECT: Lap Desk
DIMENSIONS: 3″ × 14¾″ × 19″
MATERIALS: Mahogany, rosewood
FINISH: Watco Danish oil
TIME SPENT: 60 hours
MATERIALS COST: $40

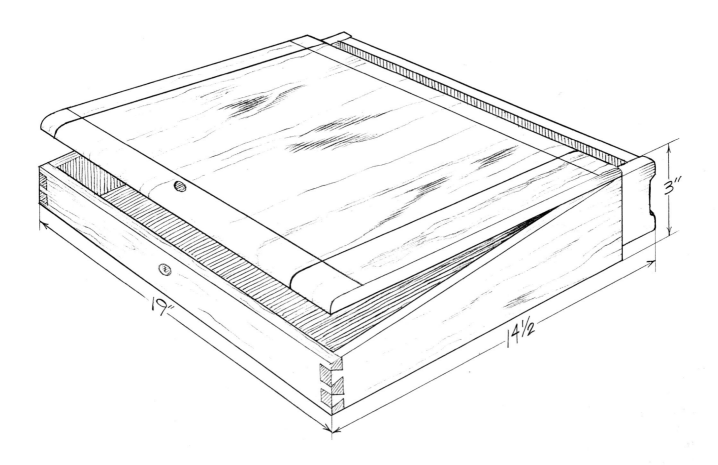

H ENRY JEX is a retired aero-
space engineer who learned to
love woodworking from his father.
This box, inspired by a Shaker lap
desk, is his master project from a fine
cabinetmaking class, as well as a
birthday gift to his wife (though it
has been widely used by family mem-
bers for the past 18 years).

PROJECT DESCRIPTION

The extended corner dovetails act as
feet to help the desk stand vertically,
like a briefcase. The open slot across
the back holds incoming and
outgoing mail and bills while you
write. The rosewood latch and
release are sprung by a hidden
stainless steel latch spring made from
a radiator clamp.

MATERIALS LIST

Lid panel (1) ⁵⁄₁₆″ × 15¼″ × 10¾″
Lid stiles (2) ½″ × 2″ × 13″
Lid rails (2) ½″ × 1½″ × 15½″
Bottom (1) ¼″ × 13½″ × 17½″
Outer back (1) ½″ × 3″ × 18″
Inner back (1) ½″ × 2¾″ × 17½″
Front divider (1) ½″ × 1½″ × 17½″
Front (1) ½″ × 1½″ × 18″
Sides (2) ½″ × 3″ × 14¼″
Long divider (1) ¼″ × 3″ × 9¾″
Short dividers (2) ¼″ × 1¾″ × 2″

Serpentine Jewelry Box

SANDOR NAGYSZALANCZY

NAME: Sandor Nagyszalanczy

HOME: Santa Cruz, California

PROJECT: Serpentine Jewelry Box

DIMENSIONS: 8″ × 8½″ × 16″

MATERIALS: Bird's-eye maple, Indian
  rosewood, Baltic birch plywood

FINISH: Nitro lacquer

TIME SPENT: 4 days

MATERIALS COST: $50

RETAIL PRICE: $500

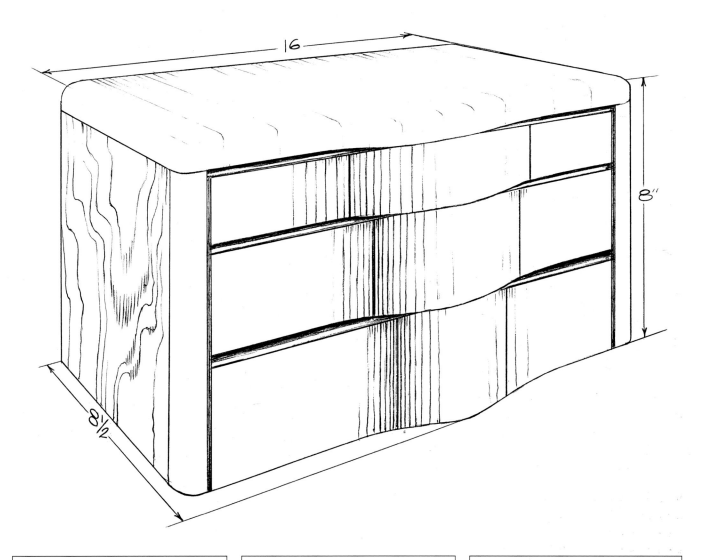

SANDOR NAGYSZALANCZY has been a professional woodworker for more than 15 years. He has built many boxes, both for commissions and gallery spec, including chests, presentation cases, jewelry boxes and cases for silver services. The inspiration for this box came from a need for a jewelry box of simple, elegant lines and one that was large enough to hold a significant amount of jewelry. 🌿

PROJECT DESCRIPTION

The serpentine drawer front is sawn to contour profile on the band saw and then sliced into individual drawer fronts. Making the drawer fronts different sizes at each level creates an interesting graphic pattern on the front.

MATERIALS LIST

Top/bottom (2) $^{11}/_{16}'' \times 8\frac{1}{2}'' \times 16''$
Sides (2) $^{11}/_{16}'' \times 7\frac{3}{4}'' \times 7\frac{5}{8}''$
Drawer front (1) $1\frac{1}{4}'' \times 7'' \times 14\frac{1}{4}''$
Drawer pull strips (3)
　$\frac{1}{4}'' \times 1\frac{1}{2}'' \times 14\frac{1}{4}''$
Side trim (2) $\frac{1}{4}'' \times \frac{3}{8}'' \times 7''$

Empire State Blanket Chest

SANDOR NAGYSZALANCZY

NAME: Sandor Nagyszalanczy

HOME: Santa Cruz, California

PROJECT: Empire State Blanket Chest

DIMENSIONS: 30″ × 26″ × 18″

MATERIALS: Red oak, red putumuju, aromatic cedar

FINISH: Nitro lacquer

TIME SPENT: 40 hours

MATERIALS COST: $100

RETAIL PRICE: $1,600

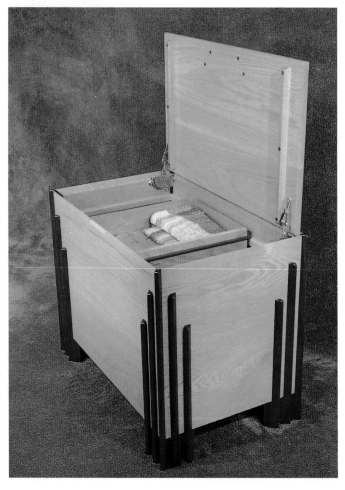

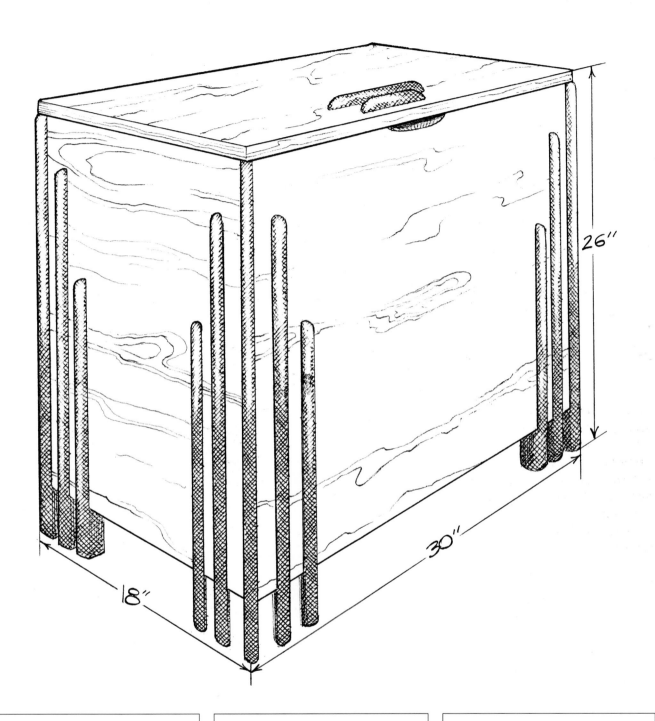

26"

30"

18"

This box was inspired by the form of the Empire State Building and Art Deco style.

PROJECT DESCRIPTION

The putumuju corner accents are set into angled grooves in the box carcass. They're only attached in the middle of the groove, so they can float, which allows for expansion and contraction of the carcass across the grain. At the bottom of the chest, the accents act as legs.

MATERIALS LIST

Top (1) ¾" × 18" × 30"
Bottom (1) ¾" × 16½" × 28½"
Sides (2) ¾" × 23" × 30"
Ends (2) ¾" × 18" × 23"
Trim (4) ¼" × ¾" × 25¼"
Trim (8) ¼" × ¾" × 22¼"
Trim (8) ¼" × ¾" × 16¼"

"Ricardo" the Penguin Jewelry Box

KURT NIELSEN

10″

6½″

35″

KURT NIELSEN is a furniture maker who has tried to incorporate "Ricardo"—a character inspired by "a childhood misspent sitting in front of Saturday morning cartoons"—in a number of pieces: tables, chairs, benches and jewelry boxes. When making a box, it is usually part of a larger piece, a "nice surprise attached to a sculpture."

PROJECT DESCRIPTION

Nielsen created the box to fit the hand-carved sculpture. The box was created to fit the sculpture proportionally.

NAME: Kurt Nielsen
HOME: Asheville, North Carolina
PROJECT: "Ricardo" the Penguin Jewelry
    Box
DIMENSIONS: Overall—15″ × 15″ × 35″;
    box—5″ × 6½″ × 10″
MATERIALS: Penguin—basswood; box—
    curly maple, maple burl, mahogany
FINISH: Acrylic paint, lacquer
MATERIALS COST: $100
RETAIL PRICE: $1,500

Ocean
JAY O BOXES

NAME: Jay O Boxes (Jay and Janet O'Rourke)
HOME: Hood River, Oregon
PROJECT: Ocean
DIMENSIONS: $10'' \times 5'' \times 3\frac{3}{4}''$
MATERIALS: Macasar ebony, pink ivorywood, black ebony
FINISH: Danish oil, carnauba wax

$3\frac{3}{4}$

5"

10"

J AY AND JANET O'ROURKE have been making boxes
since 1970. The wood itself is a major design element in
their pieces. An elegant container will make all of your trea-
sures more prized—for dreams, sacred moments, jewels and
secrets. Their work can be seen in the world's finest galleries
and museums. To them, there is a secret, mystical quality
to vessels.

Inspirations for Jay O Boxes come from a great love of
containers, ancient architecture, Asian art, Art Deco and
lately from the skies. Their work is leading them to the
future. To the O'Rourkes, woods are as rare as the finest
gold or diamonds. Working the wood from its raw form
and bringing out the beauty of the grains and colors is like
working with fine gemstones. The use of simple elegant
design is used to showcase the beautiful combinations of
high contrasting woods. ∼

PROJECT DESCRIPTION

Basically this is a band sawn box with
a turned top, legs and drawer pulls.
The mermaid is hand carved.

Rabbit Moon

JAY O BOXES

NAME: Jay O Boxes (Jay and Janet O'Rourke)
HOME: Hood River, Oregon
PROJECT: Rabbit Moon
DIMENSIONS: $10'' \times 6'' \times 4''$
MATERIALS: Black palm, snakewood, taqua nut
FINISH: Danish oil, carnauba wax

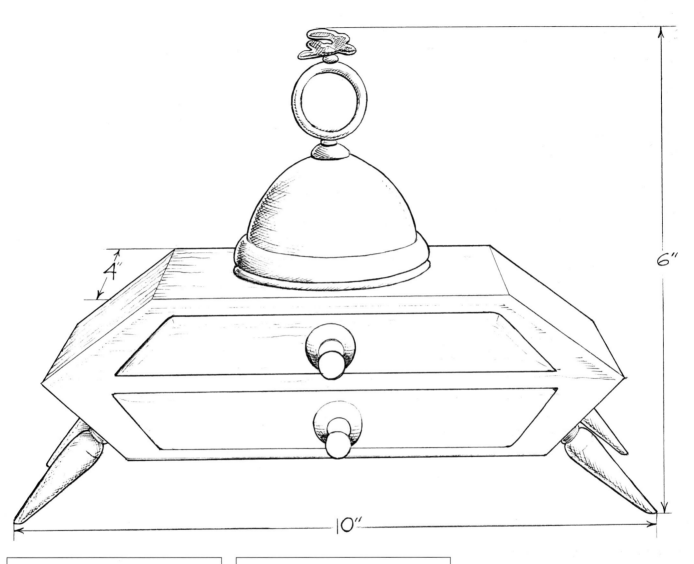

6"

4"

10"

The inspiration for the carved pieces "comes from the Goddesses."

PROJECT DESCRIPTION

This is another band sawn box with turned top, legs and drawer pulls. The carving is a turned taqua nut, and the rabbit is snakewood.

Bird of Prey

JAY O BOXES

NAME: Jay O Boxes (Jay and Janet O'Rourke)
HOME: Hood River, Oregon
PROJECT: Bird of Prey
DIMENSIONS: 12″ × 6″ × 5″
MATERIALS: Wenge, snakewood, African blackwood, palmwood
FINISH: Danish oil, carnauba wax

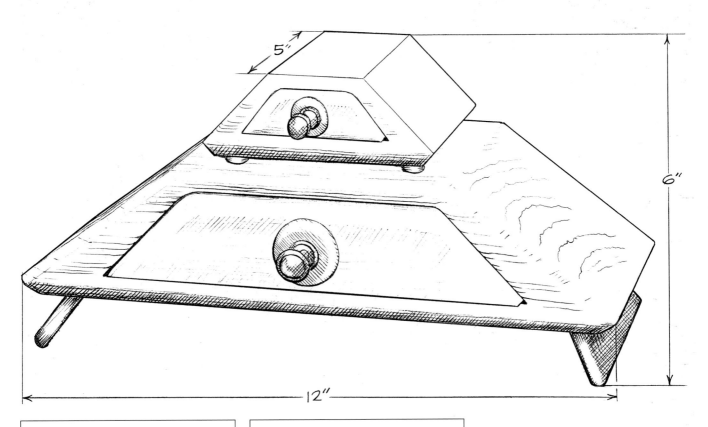

The inspiration of this piece comes from a great love of birds. ∽

This is a band sawn box with turned drawer pulls.

Retro Sleek

JAY O BOXES

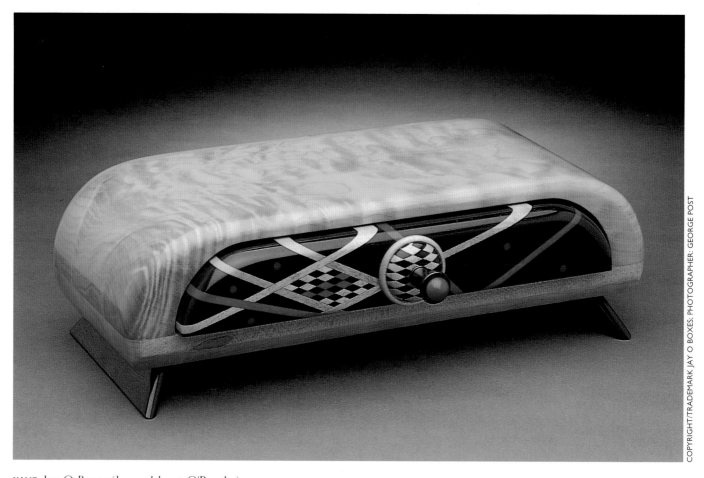

NAME: Jay O Boxes (Jay and Janet O'Rourke)
HOME: Hood River, Oregon
PROJECT: Retro Sleek
DIMENSIONS: 12″ × 6″ × 4″
MATERIALS: Curly maple, ebony, pink ivorywood
FINISH: Danish oil, carnauba wax

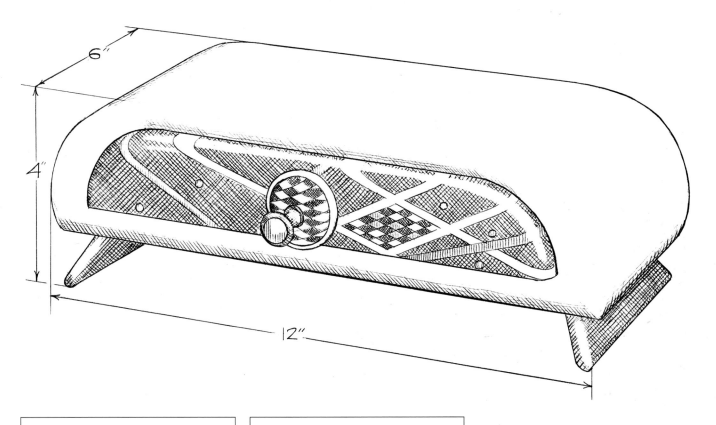

6"

4"

12"

The inspiration for this box comes from a love of the Art Deco style.

PROJECT DESCRIPTION

The drawer front of this band sawn box is laminated and inlaid. The drawer pull is laminated and turned.

Spaceship I
JAY O BOXES

NAME: Jay O Boxes (Jay and Janet O'Rourke)
HOME: Hood River, Oregon
PROJECT: Spaceship I
DIMENSIONS: 12″ × 6″ × 5½″
MATERIALS: Purpleheart, ebony, maple, pink ivorywood
FINISH: Danish oil, carnauba wax

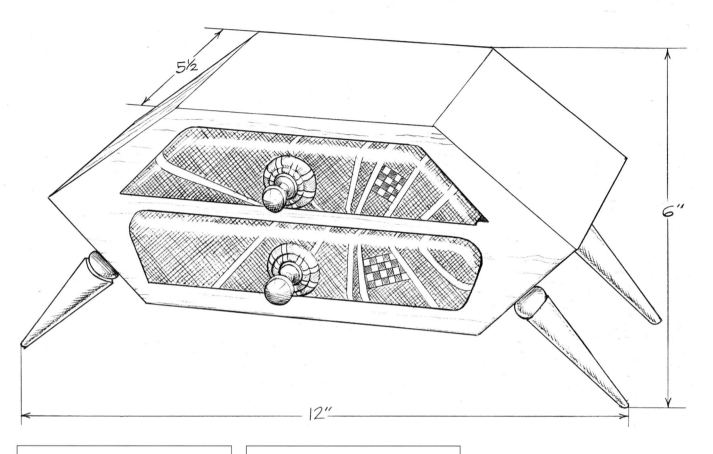

5½

6"

12"

PROJECT DESCRIPTION

This is a band sawn box with a laminated drawer front and turned drawer pulls and legs.

The Pyramid
JAY O BOXES

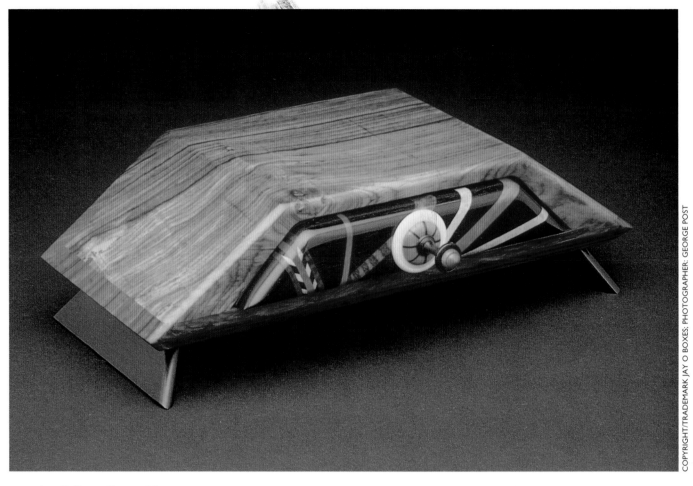

NAME: Jay O Boxes (Jay and Janet
   O'Rourke)
HOME: Hood River, Oregon
PROJECT: The Pyramid
DIMENSIONS: 12" × 6" × 4"
MATERIALS: Cocobolo, ebony, snakewood,
   pink ivorywood, maple, taqua nut
FINISH: Danish oil, carnauba wax

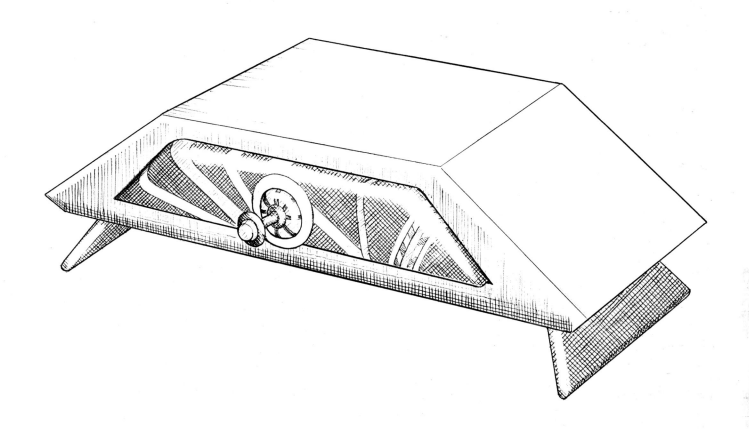

PROJECT DESCRIPTION

Laminated drawer front and turned drawer pull.

Box for Ted

MELINDA RAMOS

NAME: Melinda Ramos

HOME: Batavia, Ohio

PROJECT: Box for Ted

DIMENSIONS: 4¾″ × 11″ × 3⅞″

MATERIALS: Walnut, plywood, pigskin leather

FINISH: Deft oil

TIME SPENT: 6 hours

MATERIALS COST: $10

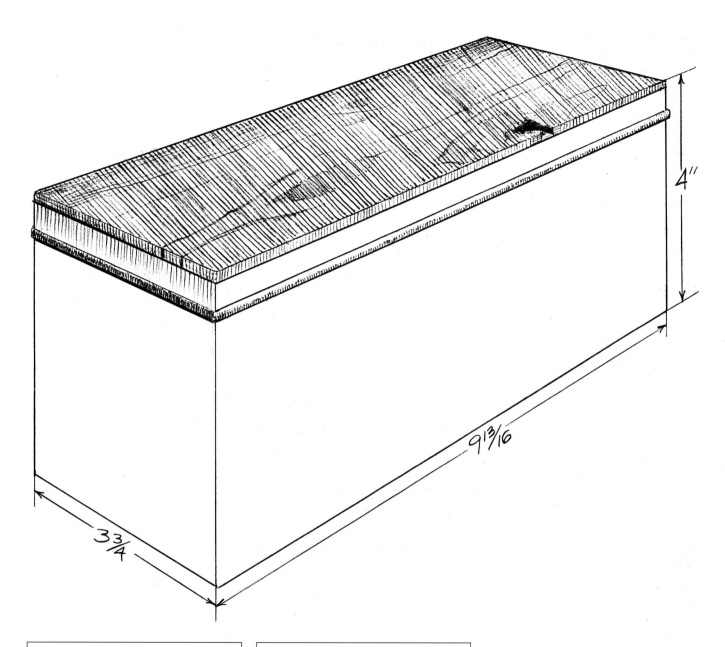

4"

9¹³⁄₁₆

3¾

MELINDA RAMOS enjoys making and collecting boxes. Though she has sold some boxes, her husband Ted is usually the recipient. In this box, she wanted to combine wood and leather. ～

MATERIALS LIST

Top (1) ¾″ × 3¾″ × 11″
Bottom (1) ¾″ × 2¾″ × 9¹³⁄₁₆″
Sides (2) ½″ × 4″ × 11″
Ends (2) ½″ × 4″ × 2¾″
Side trim (2) ⅛″ × 11″ × ⅜″
End trim (2) ⅛″ × 3¾″ × ⅜″

Another Box for Ted

MELINDA RAMOS

NAME: Melinda Ramos
HOME: Batavia, Ohio
PROJECT: Another Box for Ted
DIMENSIONS: 5⅝″ × 3¾″ × 3¾″
MATERIALS: Cherry, maple
FINISH: Deft oil
TIME SPENT: 4 hours
MATERIALS COST: scrap

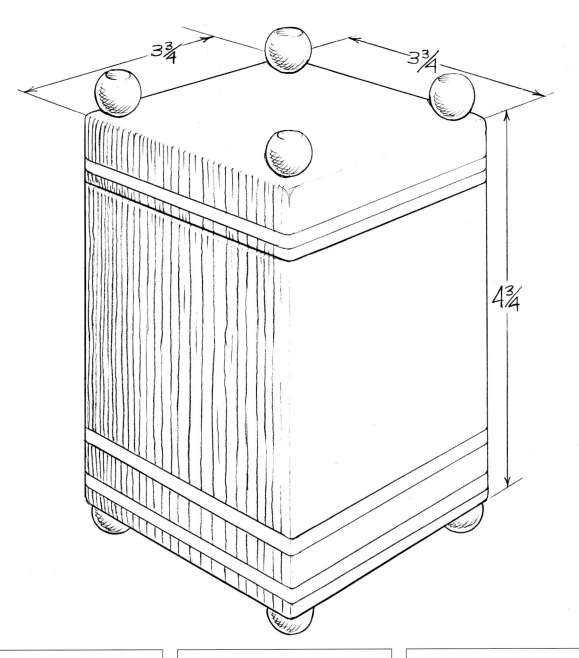

$3\frac{3}{4}$

$3\frac{3}{4}$

$4\frac{3}{4}$

T his project is the beginning effort of working through a box of cherry scraps left over from previous work. ⌒

PROJECT DESCRIPTION

The chunk of cherry is cut across its top to release the piece to become the lid. Then the center is cut out with a hole saw. Cut the bottom off the chunk to release the center portion; then fill this kerf with inlay. Cut away the lip of the lid so that the center portion of the lid fits the center of the box. Finally, add the dowels and matching holes to keep the lid registered squarely.

MATERIALS LIST

One piece $3\frac{3}{4}'' \times 3\frac{3}{4}'' \times 4\frac{3}{4}''$

Pyramid Jewelry Box

MELINDA RAMOS

NAME: Melinda Ramos
HOME: Batavia, Ohio
PROJECT: Pyramid Jewelry Box
DIMENSIONS: 11⅛″ × 10¼″ × 7⅝″
MATERIALS: Cherry, poplar
FINISH: Deft oil
TIME SPENT: 30 hours
MATERIALS COST: $20

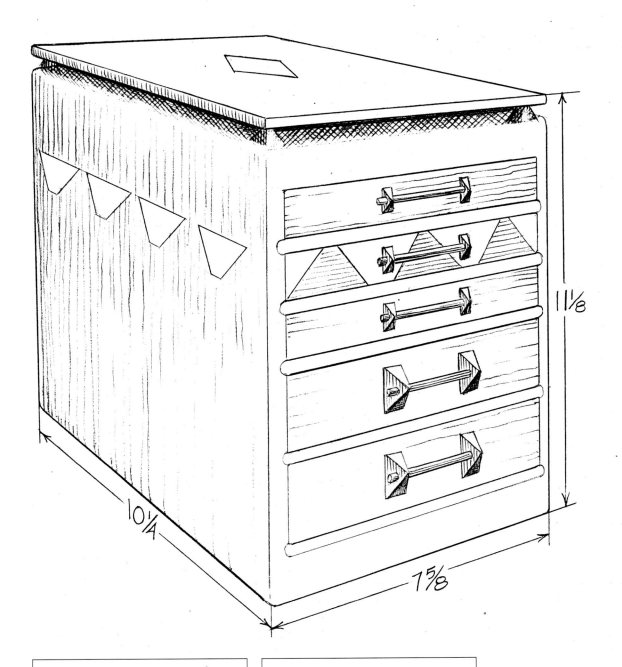

10¼

11⅛

7⅝

"Pyramids are sentimental to my husband and me; we just like the shape. One day while I was taking a walk, this box formed itself in my mind. Working my way through it was another matter. My husband was helpful with some rather sticky problems!" ⌒

PROJECT DESCRIPTION

This is a complicated piece. There are many pieces, five drawers (with pyramid and dowel pulls), pyramid feet and a floating shelf.

Shaker Surprise

RALPH SPRANG

NAME: Ralph Sprang

HOME: Milford, Ohio

PROJECT: Shaker Surprise

DIMENSIONS: 1³⁄₁₆″ diameter × 1⁷⁄₁₆″ high

MATERIALS: Cherry

FINISH: Shellac, wax

TIME SPENT: 2 hours

MATERIALS COST: $3

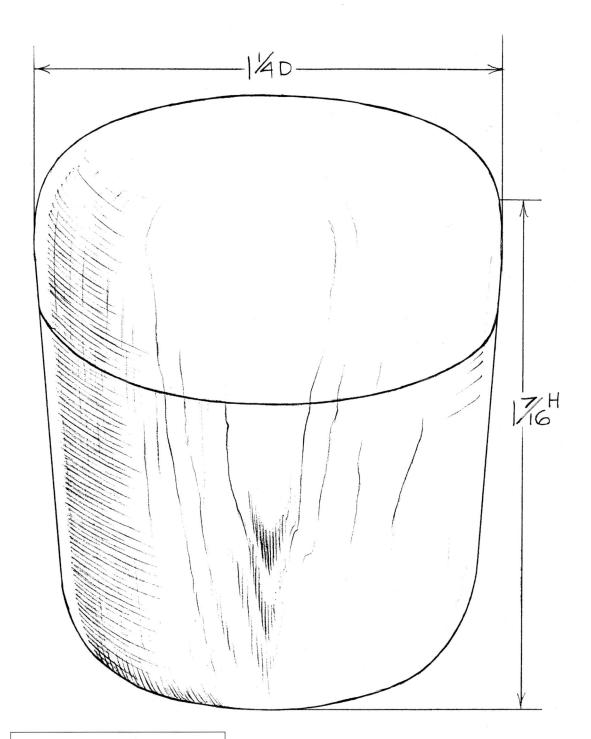

1¼D

1⁷⁄₁₆H

R ALPH SPRANG has been doing
serious woodturning since he
was 16. The Shaker ideals of simplicity in life and simplicity in design are
the inspiration for this tiny box.

Heart Box

JOHN SWANSON

NAME: John Swanson

HOME: Renton, Washington

PROJECT: Heart Box

DIMENSIONS: $11'' \times 8'' \times 6''$

MATERIALS: Walnut, maple, redheart

FINISH: Sanding sealer, Hydrocote

TIME SPENT: 6 hours

MATERIALS COST: $15

RETAIL PRICE: $50

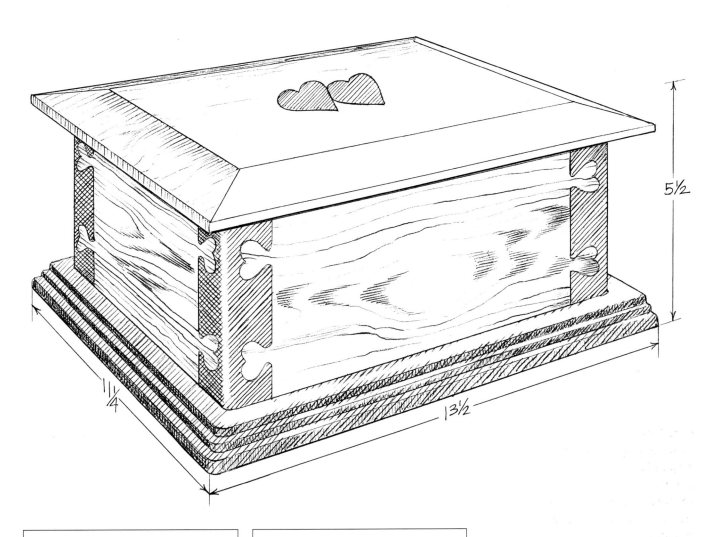

5½

11¼

13½

J OHN SWANSON is a retired
pilot/design engineer from
Boeing. He has been an amateur
woodworker for 35 years. Swanson
built this box for holding small arti-
cles on his wife's dresser. 〜

MATERIALS LIST

Sides (2) ¼″ × 4″ × 9″
Ends (2) ¼″ × 4″ × 6″
Corners (4) 1″ × 1″ × 4″
Base molding ¾″ × 2″ × 40″
Base insert ¼″ × 5″ × 9″ plywood
Top ½″ × 8″ × 11″
Walnut lid inlay (2) ½″ × ⅜″ × 11″
Redheart lid inlay (1) ½″ × ½″ × 11″

Turned Boxes

JOHN SWANSON

NAME: John Swanson

HOME: Renton, Washington

PROJECT: Turned Boxes

DIMENSIONS: Various diameters and heights

MATERIALS: Myrtlewood, apple, maple burl, spalted maple, cocobolo, banksia pod

FINISH: Various (tung oil, wax, Behr Clear Lac, Liberon wax)

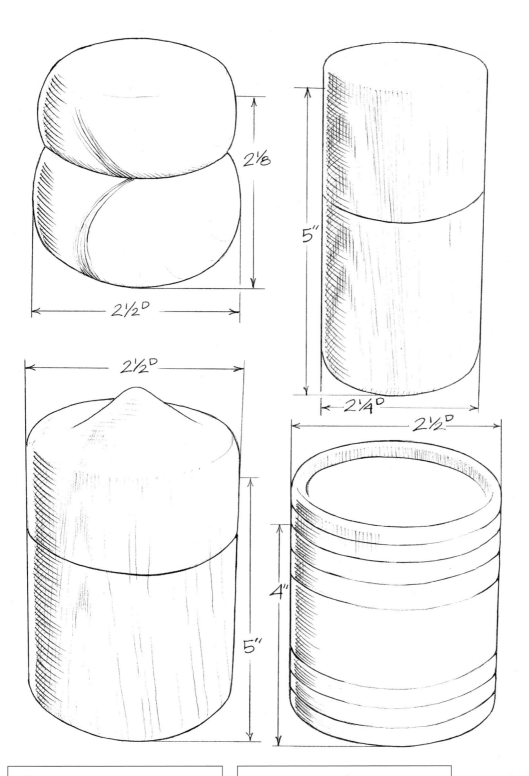

2⅛

2½ᴰ

5"

2¼ᴰ

2½ᴰ

2½ᴰ

5"

4"

J OHN SWANSON has only been
turning wood for a few years.
After each of a number of classes he
has taken, Swanson has turned a box
as a way of putting what he's learned
into practice. ◞

PROJECT DESCRIPTION

Some of the boxes have threaded lids
made with a jig that Swanson got
from a Bonnie Klein class.

Secrets
DAVID TERPENING

NAME: David Terpening

HOME: Charlotte, North Carolina

PROJECT: Secrets

DIMENSIONS: 12″ × 6″ × 6″

MATERIALS: African wenge, pink spalted dogwood

FINISH: Watco Danish Oil, Barclay gel varnish

TIME SPENT: 3 hours

MATERIALS COST: $15

RETAIL PRICE: $350

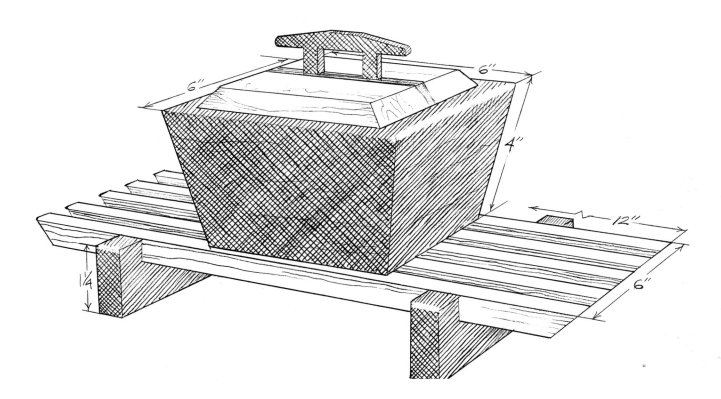

With this one-of-a-kind piece, David Terpening tried to create "an aura of mystery." While there is an impulse to lift the lid and look inside, our better judgment tells us its contents are secret, for the eyes of the owner only.

PROJECT DESCRIPTION

The box sides are mitered together; the most difficult aspect of doing this is determining the angle at which the sides should be cut to get 6" at the top and 4" along the bottom. Also, the spalted dogwood is hard to find because it develops its characteristics while standing for a long time after the tree has died.

MATERIALS LIST

Sides (4) 4" × 6" × 1⅛"
Bottom (1) ¼" × 3⅞" × 3⅞" plywood
Lid sides (2) ½" × 2³⁄₁₆" × 4¾"
Lid center (1) ½" × ⅜" × 4¾"
Handle (1) ⅜" × ⅜" × 3¾"
Handle posts (2) ⅜" × ⅜" × ½"
Base feet (2) ⅞" × 1½" × 6"
Base slats (6) ½" × ½" × 12"

The Empress Collection

DAVID TERPENING

NAME: David Terpening
HOME: Charlotte, North Carolina
PROJECT: The Empress Collection
DIMENSIONS: 6½″ × 3½″ × 2″
MATERIALS: Wenge, maple veneer and various exotics
FINISH: Watco Danish oil, Barclay gel varnish
TIME SPENT: 3 hours
MATERIALS COST: $15-$20
RETAIL PRICE: $150-$180

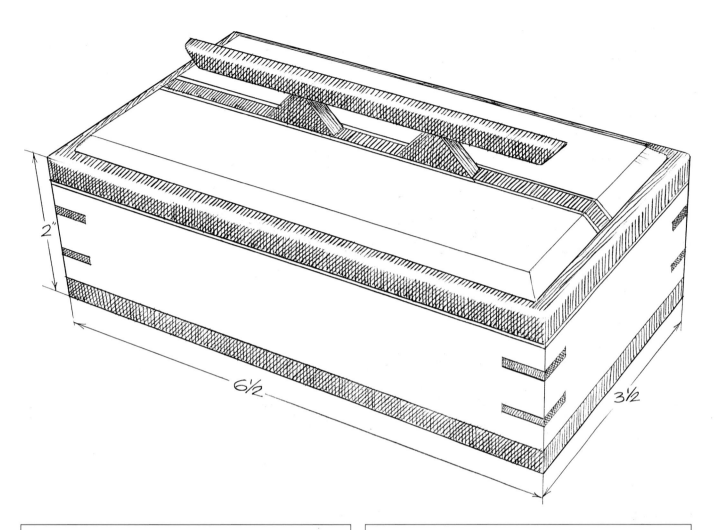

2"

6½

3½

DAVID TERPENING has been involved with wood-working in one form or another since childhood when he began in his father's basement shop. As an adult, and being confined to apartment living, he began working with veneers and inlays, eventually becoming proficient in marquetry. Today, David concentrates on finely detailed ornamental boxes. He enjoys combining different species of woods and veneers to produce dramatic effects.

With this box, he says, "I wanted to design a box that would appeal to a woman, that would draw her to it with a desire to touch and hold the piece. I wanted to design a handle that would demand the observer to lift it, to impart curiosity. I wanted the piece to be delicate, yet large enough to hold a necklace or other valuables. I wanted the piece to be tasteful, thus the laminations of wenge and maple."

MATERIALS LIST

Ends (2) 3½″ × 1¼″ × 5⁄16″
Sides (2) 6½″ × 1¼″ × 5⁄16″
Side lamination (4) 6½″ × 5⁄16″ × 5⁄16″
End lamination (4) 3½″ × 5⁄16″ × 5⁄16″
Splines (8) 2″ × ¾″ × ⅛″

PROJECT DESCRIPTION

There is nothing unusual or unique for practicing box makers in this box. However, the lamination for the sides and ends is a bit of a different approach to box making.

Harvard Jewelry Box
PETER TURNER

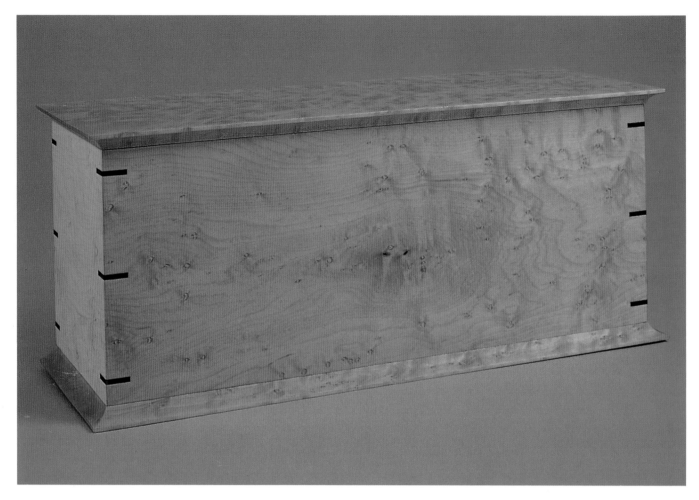

NAME: Peter Turner

HOME: Maine

PROJECT: Harvard Jewelry Box

DIMENSIONS: 19½″ × 7½″ × 8½″

MATERIALS: Bird's-eye maple, Granadillo

FINISH: Livos, Dubno primer and Kaldet top coat

TIME SPENT: 12-15 hours

MATERIALS COST: $52

RETAIL PRICE: $550

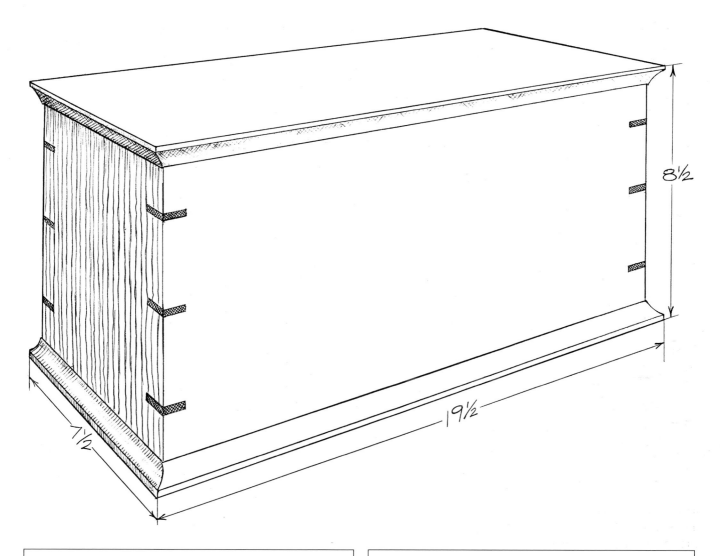

P ETER TURNER is a self-trained woodworker who works mostly in traditional American design. Most of Turner's designs begin as gifts for his wife. For this box, Turner was inspired by a candle box he saw in an antique store on Harvard Street in Brookline, Massachusetts, hence the name. The four interior trays provide storage for small pieces with ample space between, for access to a larger lower stash. ⌐

PROJECT DESCRIPTION

The miters of this box are cut so that figure wraps around three corners, then strengthened with contrasting cross splines. The one-piece base is screwed to the box through a hole (at the front) and slots (middle and back) to allow for wood movement.

MATERIALS LIST
_____

Top (1) 7¾″ × 20½″ × ½″
Base (1) 7¾″ × 20½″ × ½″
Front/Back (2) 7″ × 19½″ × ½″
Sides (2) 7″ × 7¼″ × ½″
Top cleats (2) ½″ × 5½″ × 9⁄16″
Upper tray supports (2) 1³⁄16″ × 18½″ × ¼″
Lower tray supports (2) ¾″ × 18½″ × ¼″
Box bottom (1) ⅛″ × 6¼″ × 18⁷⁄16″ plywood
Upper tray sides (4) 1¹⁄16″ × 6⅛″ × ¼″
Lower tray sides (4) 1¹⁄16″ × 5⅝″ × ¼″
Tray ends (8) 1¹⁄16″ × 4⁷⁄16″ × ¼″
Upper tray dividers (2) ¾″ × 5¹¹⁄16″ × ¼″
Lower tray dividers (2) ¾″ × 5¹⁄16″ × ¼″
Tray crosspieces (4) 9⁄16″ × 4³⁄16″ × ⅛″
Upper tray bottoms (2) 4⅜″ × 5¹³⁄16″ × ⅛″ plywood
Lower tray bottoms (2) 4⅜″ × 5⁵⁄16″ × ⅛″ plywood

Crutch Box

RANDY COOK WORKS

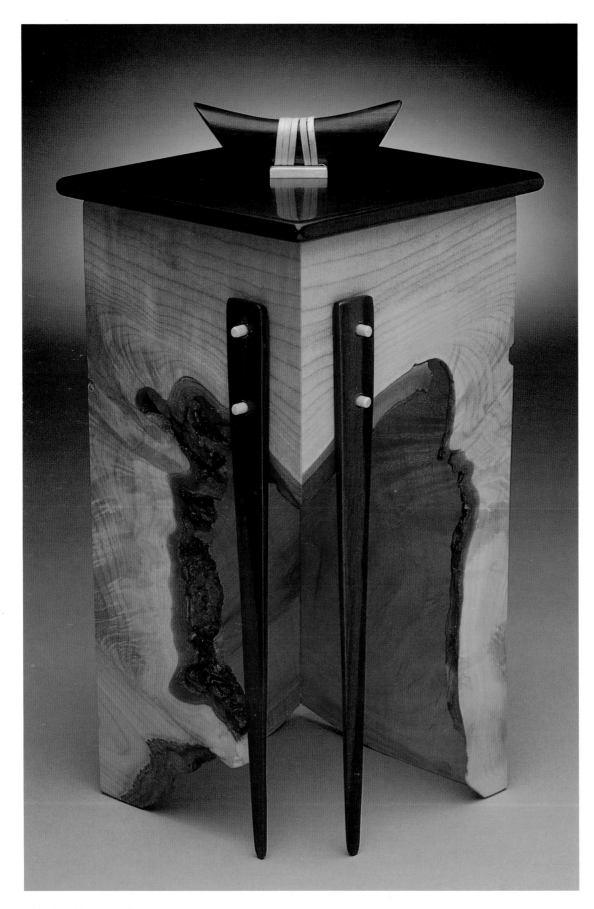

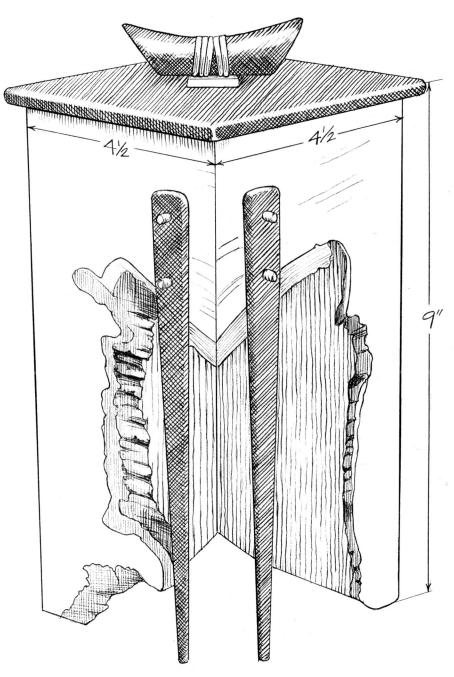

4½

4½

9″

RANDY COOK has been making boxes in his own distinguished style for most of the past decade. This box was inspired by a memory of a sports injury: "Years ago I screwed up my ankles playing sports, so I was on crutches. When I saw this wood, I thought it needed a little help with some crutches."

NAME: Randy Cook Works (Randy Cook)
HOME: Long Beach, Washington
PROJECT: Crutch Box
DIMENSIONS: 4½″ × 4½″ × 9″
MATERIALS: Western maple, rosewood, Ebon-X
FINISH: Varnish, oil, wax
TIME SPENT: 6 hours
RETAIL PRICE: $245

Leather/Ebony

RANDY COOK WORKS

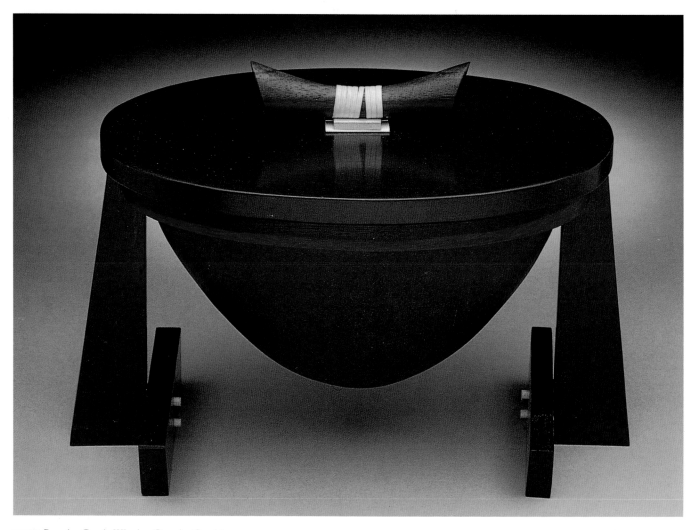

NAME: Randy Cook Works (Randy Cook)

HOME: Long Beach, Washington

PROJECT: Leather/Ebony

DIMENSIONS: 6″ × 8″ × 7″

MATERIALS: Ebon-X, ebony, ebony veneer, alder

FINISH: Varnish, wax

TIME SPENT: 12 hours

RETAIL PRICE: $625

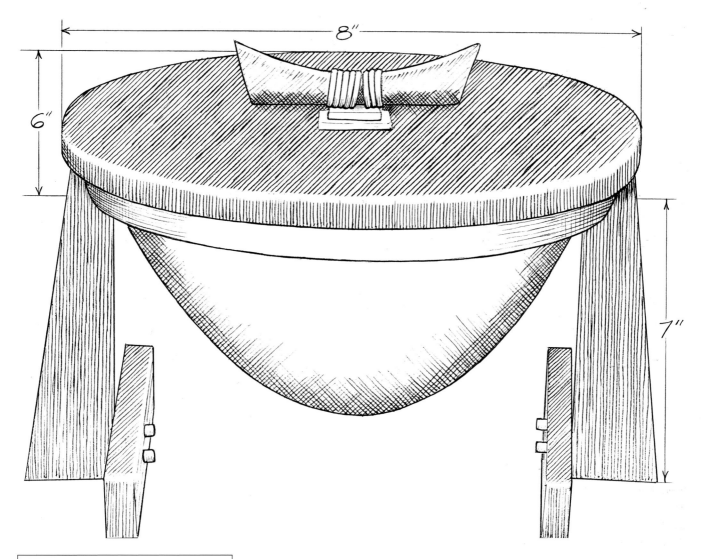

8"

6"

7"

Using boiled and form-pounded leather, Randy Cook does a take-off from leather helmet making in this design. It is an interesting composition with a unique transition from hard to soft.

Montana Box

RANDY COOK WORKS

NAME: Randy Cook Works (Randy Cook)

HOME: Long Beach, Washington

PROJECT: Montana Box

DIMENSIONS: $4\frac{1}{2}'' \times 7'' \times 6''$

MATERIALS: Rosewood, western maple, Ebon-X

FINISH: Varnish, oil, wax

TIME SPENT: 5 hours

RETAIL PRICE: $195

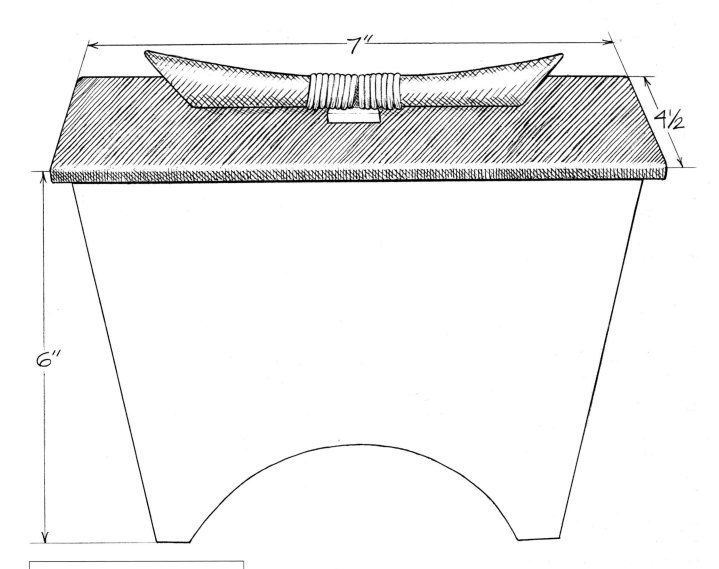

RANDY COOK thinks of all his boxes as shapes, as simple containers—not by utility. This box is named for the home state of one of Randy's helpers.

Laminated Heart Boxes

KERRY VESPER

NAME: Kerry Vesper

HOME: Tempe, Arizona

PROJECT: Laminated Heart Boxes

DIMENSIONS: 7″ × 7″ × 2½″

MATERIALS: Walnut, cherry, Baltic birch

TIME SPENT: 5 hours

MATERIALS COST: $10

RETAIL PRICE: $200

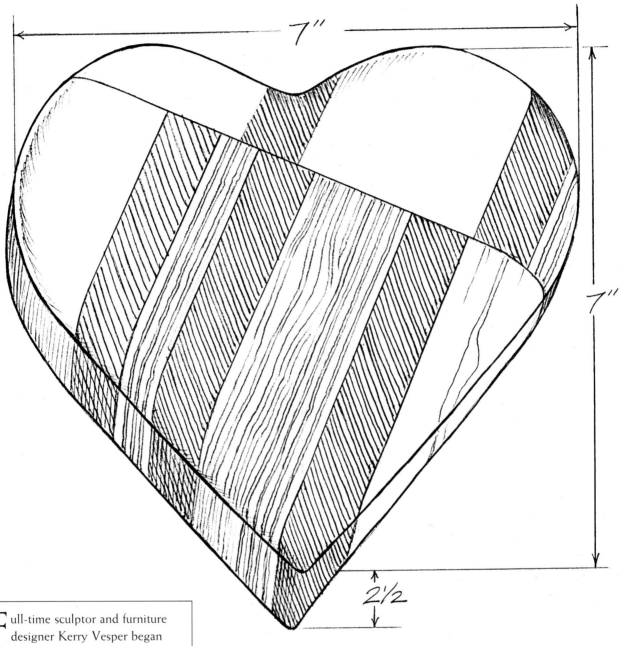

7"

7"

2½

Full-time sculptor and furniture designer Kerry Vesper began carving wood in the early 1970s. As he became more interested in abstract sculpture, instead of ducks, birds, animals, etc., he began laminating different kinds of wood together to carve. The heart designs began as smaller valentines for his wife, and then he used them for birthday and wedding gifts. Eventually he realized that the hearts could be made larger and cut to form boxes.

Treasure Chest

THOMAS TANGIBLES

NAME: Thomas Tangibles (Carl Thomas)

HOME: Amelia, Ohio

PROJECT: Treasure Chest

DIMENSIONS: 11¾″ × 9¾″ × 8¼″

MATERIALS: Wormy maple, oak, birch plywood

FINISH: Deft Semi-Gloss Clear Wood Finish

TIME SPENT: 3 hours

MATERIALS COST: $15

RETAIL PRICE: $65

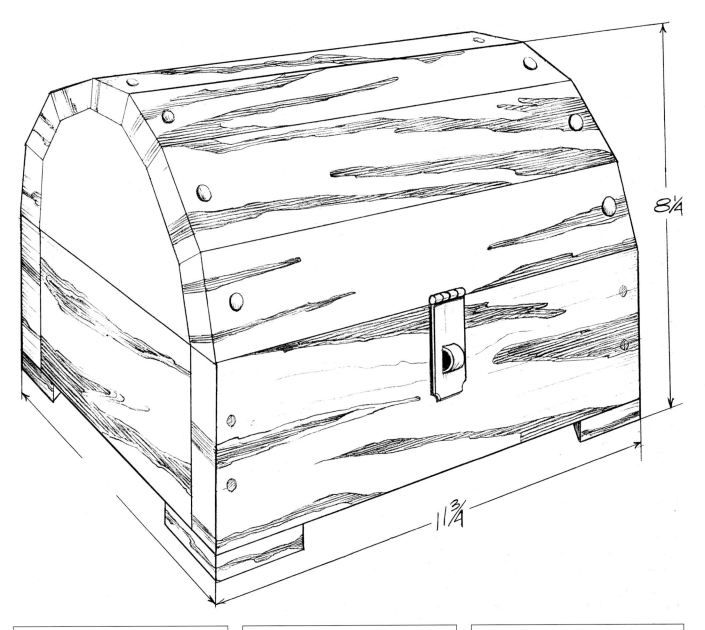

8¼

11¾

CARL THOMAS originally
made turned craft show items
(bowls, vases, lazy Susans, etc.).
However, many of his customers began asking for fancy boxes. This box
was inspired by childhood memories
of reading about pirates and treasure
chests.

PROJECT DESCRIPTION

Cut the seven top pieces on your
table saw set at 20°. To glue the top
pieces together to form the semi-
circle lid, hold them with tape until
the glue dries. The glued-up top is
held to the ends using dowels.

MATERIALS LIST

Top (7) ¾" × 2" × 11¾"
Top ends (2) ¾" × 3½" × 8½"
Bottom ends (2) ¾" × 3½" × 8½"
Bottom front pieces (2)
    ¾" × 3½" × 11¾"
Box bottom (1) ¼" × 8¼" × 10¼"
    plywood
Feet (4) 2" × 2" × 2¾"

Colonial-Style Candle Box

ANDERS HANDCRAFTS

NAME: Anders Handcrafts (Maurice Anders)

HOME: Oklahoma City, Oklahoma

PROJECT: Colonial-Style Candle Box

DIMENSIONS: 4″ × 8″ × 12″

MATERIALS: Cherry

FINISH: Shellac

TIME SPENT: 30 hours

MATERIALS COST: $25

RETAIL PRICE: $200

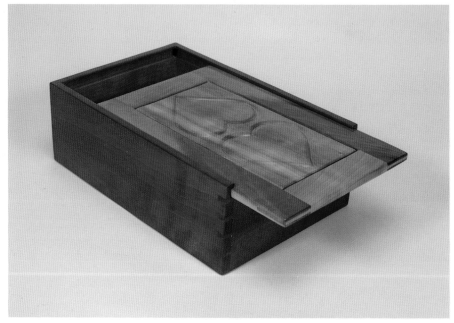

This box is reminiscent of the candle boxes popular during the colonial days. Rather than make authentic reproductions, I prefer to get ideas from classic pieces and modify the design or construction to suit my taste. Some of the colonial boxes were constructed with a single board that slid in and out of grooves in the sides. The lid quite often stuck during humid conditions and occasionally warped and didn't slide easily. To avoid the sticky lid syndrome, I built the lid using a frame and panel construction. The frame for the lid is joined by open mortise and tenon joints. The lid can be reversed with hearts on one side and a plain panel on the opposite side. I don't store many candles, but I find the box very useful for storing photographs. ⌇

MATERIALS LIST

Lid panel (1) ⅜″ × 5¼″ × 9½″
Lid frame sides (2) ⅜″ × 1½″ × 11¾″
Lid frame ends (2) ⅜″ × 1½″ × 7½″
Box bottom (1) ⅜″ × 8⅛″ × 11¾″
Box sides (2) ⅜″ × 4″ × 12″
Box ends (2) ⅜″ × 4″ × 8″

PROJECT DESCRIPTION

The box is joined with hand-cut dovetails. I used shellac to finish the box because I prefer the aroma of shellac to other finishes. The aroma of the finish of the inside of the box will last a long time and may permeate the contents of the box.

Playing Card Boxes
ANDERS HANDCRAFTS

NAME: Anders Handcrafts (Maurice Anders)

HOME: Oklahoma City, Oklahoma

PROJECT: Playing Card Boxes

DIMENSIONS: Single deck—1¾″ × 3¼″ × 4¼″; double deck—1¾″ × 4¼″ × 6¼″

MATERIALS: Walnut, cherry, purpleheart or maple

FINISH: Lacquer

TIME SPENT: 4-6 hours

MATERIALS COST: $7

RETAIL PRICE: $40-$60

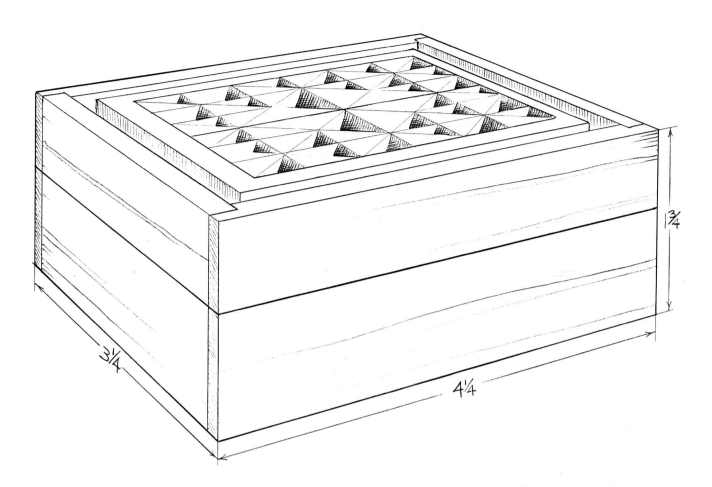

Some people are satisfied with leaving a deck of playing cards in their original cardboard box, but not Maurice Anders. His preference is to build an attractive box and use it as a decorative accent piece. Anders's chip carving is a means of enhancing a plain box; he uses geometric designs frequently, but a monogram makes the box a very personal gift. ✎

PROJECT DESCRIPTION

Before the box is glued together, rout a groove (about half the thickness of the piece) around the inside of the end and side pieces. This will be the lower edge of the top. After the box is glued together, rout a groove around the outside edge of the box so that the edge of the groove will meet the edge of the groove on the inside. This allows the bottom and top to be separated and forms a lip around the bottom where the lid fits over.

MATERIALS LIST

Single Deck
Top/bottom (2) ¼″ × 3³⁄₁₆″ × 3¹⁵⁄₁₆″
Sides (2) ¼″ × 2″ × 4¼″
Ends (2) ¼″ × 2″ × 4″

Double Deck
Top/bottom (2) ¼″ × 4³⁄₁₆″ × 5¹⁵⁄₁₆″
Sides (2) ¼″ × 2″ × 6¼″
Ends (2) ¼″ × 2″ × 4″

File Card Box

ANDERS HANDCRAFTS

NAME: Anders Handcrafts (Maurice Anders)

HOME: Oklahoma City, Oklahoma

PROJECT: File Card Box

DIMENSIONS: $4'' \times 4'' \times 5\frac{5}{8}''$

MATERIALS: Walnut, basswood

FINISH: Lacquer

TIME SPENT: 5 hours to make the box; 4 hours to carve the lid

MATERIALS COST: $6

RETAIL PRICE: $60

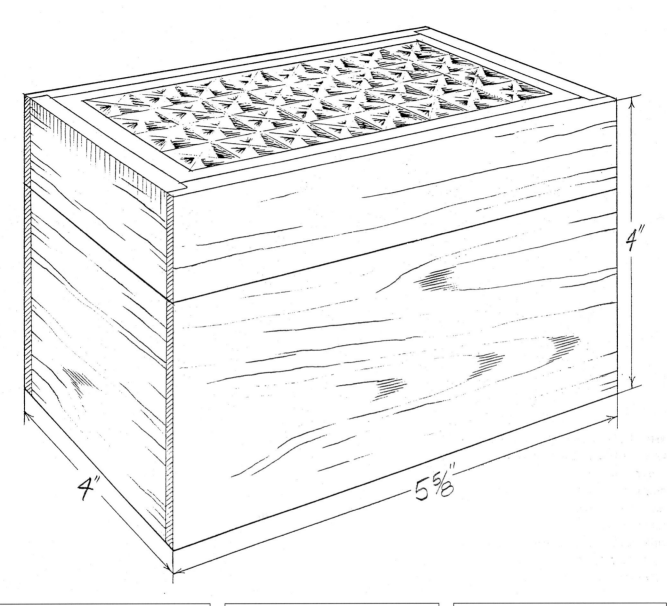

4"

4"

5⅝"

F or Maurice Anders, containers are fascinating and challenging. "Part of the challenge is to design and construct a container more useful, more unique or more beautiful than any I have done before." Most of Anders's boxes are for specific purposes: "I believe that designing a box for a specific purpose improves the utilitarian function. I enjoy owning and using a box that incorporates utility and beauty and it all works together." This box was designed to hold recipe cards or computer disks.

PROJECT DESCRIPTION

The sides and ends are cut out of a single piece of walnut so that the grain would flow continuously around the box. The board must be wide enough for the lid and bottom and a little extra, because the box is glued together and then the top is cut from the bottom on the table saw.

MATERIALS LIST

Top (1) ¼" × 3¾" × 5⅜"
Bottom (1) ¼" × 3¾" × 5⅜"
Sides (2) ¼" × 4" × 5⅝"
Ends (2) ¼" × 4" × 3¾"

Computer Disk Boxes
ANDERS HANDCRAFTS

NAME: Anders Handcrafts (Maurice
   Anders)
HOME: Oklahoma City, Oklahoma
PROJECT: Computer Disk Boxes
DIMENSIONS: $5'' \times 5'' \times 9\frac{1}{8}''$
MATERIALS: Walnut, basswood
FINISH: Lacquer
TIME SPENT: 6 hours to make the box; 6
   hours to carve the top
MATERIALS COST: $17
RETAIL PRICE: $75

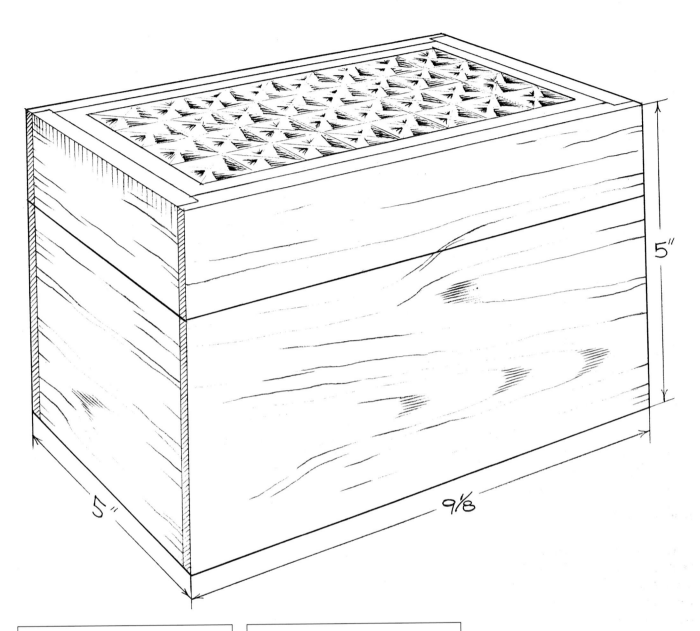

5″

9⅛

5″

The idea behind this project was to create a box that would hold regular 3½″ computer disks and would look elegant enough to fit in an executive office.

MATERIALS LIST

Top (1) ¼″ × 4¾″ × 8¾″
Bottom (1) ¼″ × 4¾″ × 8¾″
Sides (2) ¼″ × 5″ × 9″
Ends (2) ¼″ × 5″ × 4¾″
Divider (1) ¼″ × 2⅜″ × 4¾″

Box for Coasters
ANDERS HANDCRAFTS

NAME: Anders Handcrafts (Maurice
Anders)

HOME: Oklahoma City, Oklahoma

PROJECT: Box for Coasters

DIMENSIONS: 2″ × 5″ × 5″

MATERIALS: Walnut, basswood

FINISH: Lacquer

TIME SPENT: 4 hours to make the box; 6
hours to carve the coasters

MATERIALS COST: $7

RETAIL PRICE: $65

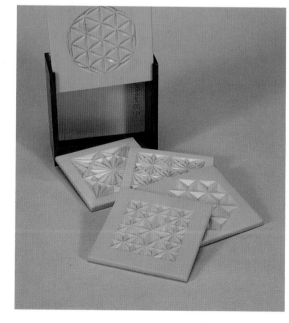

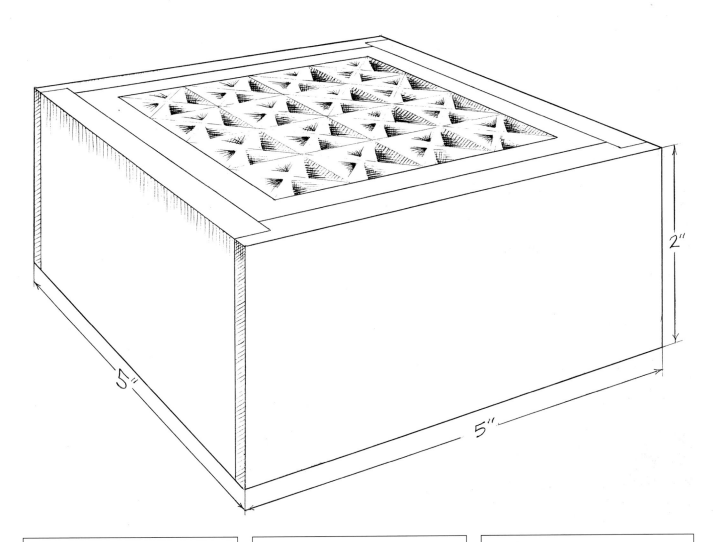

This box is the answer to the desire to build a box that would hold coasters and be attractive.

PROJECT DESCRIPTION

This box is constructed with grooves in the sides so the top and bottom slide in and out and can be used as additional coasters.

MATERIALS LIST

Top/bottom (2) ¼" × 4½" × 4⅜"
Front (1) ¼" × 1¼" × 4½"
Back (1) ¼" × 2" × 4½"
Sides (2) ¼" × 2" × 4¾"
Coasters (4) ¼" × 4" × 4"

Playing Card Box

KEITH MEALY

NAME: Keith Mealy
HOME: Cincinnati, Ohio
PROJECT: Playing Card Box
DIMENSIONS: $5^{13}/_{16}'' \times 4^{9}/_{16}'' \times 1^{5}/_{8}''$
MATERIALS: Walnut, bird's-eye maple
FINISH: Danish oil, wax
TIME SPENT: 3 hours

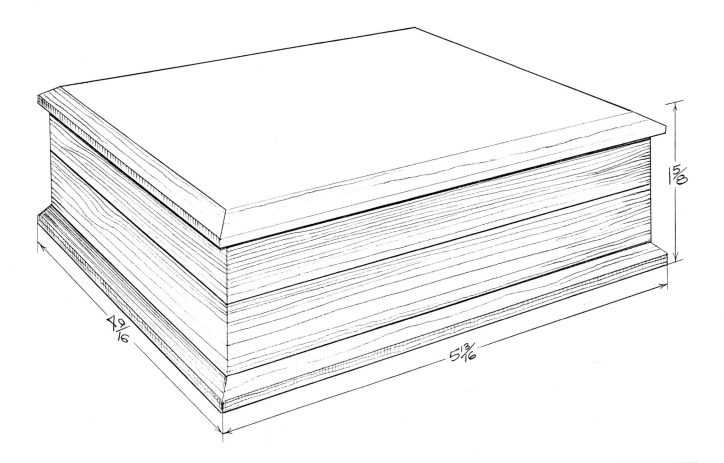

$4\frac{9}{16}$

$5\frac{13}{16}$

$1\frac{5}{8}$

K EITH MEALY, a technical
manager for a computer soft-
ware company, is a hobbyist woodworker whose interests include furniture making, finishing, carving and
box making. This box is scaled to
hold two decks of standard bridge
playing cards; since dimensions of
cards vary, the box was built to accommodate a particular deck. 〜

PROJECT DESCRIPTION

This box was made by resawing and
bookmatching both top and sides.
The top is a simple two-way
bookmatch; the sides are matched so
the grain wraps around all four
corners.

MATERIALS LIST

Top (1) $4\frac{1}{4}'' \times 5\frac{3}{8}'' \times \frac{3}{8}''$
Bottom (1) $4\frac{1}{4}'' \times 5\frac{3}{8}'' \times \frac{1}{4}''$ plywood
Sides (2) $\frac{1}{4}'' \times 1\frac{3}{8}'' \times 5\frac{13}{16}''$
Ends (2) $\frac{1}{4}'' \times 1\frac{3}{8}'' \times 4\frac{9}{16}''$
Liner $\frac{1}{8}'' \times \frac{11}{16}'' \times 16''$ cut to fit

JFK Humidor Replica

POPULAR WOODWORKING MAGAZINE

NAME: *Popular Woodworking* Magazine
    (David Thiel, Associate Editor)
HOME: Cincinnati, Ohio
PROJECT: JFK Humidor Replica
DIMENSIONS: 17¼" × 10¼" × 10½"
MATERIALS: Walnut, Spanish cedar
FINISH: Lacquer
TIME SPENT: 40 hours
MATERIALS COST: Less than $300 (including
    humidifier, hygrometer and hardware)

This humidor was a project in the July 1997 issue of *Popular Woodworking* magazine. Taking photos and dimensions of the exterior, Associate Editor David Thiel extrapolated scant information into a ⅞ replica of the original humidor given to President Kennedy by Milton Berle, which was sold at auction for $574,000. Although explained and constructed as a humidor, this elegant walnut box makes a wonderful jewelry box.

PROJECT DESCRIPTION

Finding pieces of walnut 11″ wide is difficult, so Thiel resawed and bookmatched a 6″ piece of 4/4 stock. Instead of cutting new pieces for the drawer fronts, he used the pieces cut from the front piece. Also, the top "drawer" in the piece is actually a false drawer front to balance the face; it was cut with a disc on a hand-held multi-tool. The box joints were cut using a lock miter joint router bit.

MATERIALS LIST

Front (1) ⅜″ × 11⅛″ × 17¼″ walnut
Back (1) ⅜″ × 10⅝″ × 17¼″ walnut
Sides (2) ⅜″ × 10⅝″ × 10¼″ walnut
Top (1) ⅜″ × 10¼″ × 17¼″ walnut
Bottom (1) ¼″ × 9⅞″ × 16⅞″ Masonite
Top and Bottom Liners (4) ⅜″ × 4¼″ × 16½″ cedar
Back Liners (2) ¼″ × 4¹⁄₁₆″ × 16½″ cedar
Front Liner (1) ¼″ × 3³⁄₁₆″ × 16½″ cedar
Bottom side liners (2) ¼″ × 2⅜″ × 9½″ cedar
Middle side liners (2) ¼″ × 2⅛″ × 9½″ cedar
Upper side liners (2) ¼″ × 3⅛″ × 9½″ cedar
Drawer runners (4) ¼″ × ¾″ × 9¼″ cedar
Lid front/back liners (2) ¼″ × ¾″ × 16½″ cedar
Lid side liners (2) ¼″ × ¾″ × 9½″ cedar
Tray front and back (2) ¼″ × 2⅞″ × 15¹⁵⁄₁₆″ cedar
Tray sides (2) ¼″ × 2⅞″ × 8¹¹⁄₁₆″ cedar
Tray bottoms (2) ¼″ × 4¼″ × 15⅝″ cedar
Drawer fronts (2) ⅜″ × 1⅞″ × 16⅛″ walnut
Drawer sides (4) ¼″ × 1⅞″ × 9⅛″ cedar
Drawer backs (2) ¼″ × 1⅞″ × 15¾″ cedar
Drawer bottoms (4) ¼″ × 4⁷⁄₁₆″ × 15¹¹⁄₁₆″ cedar
Front/back mouldings (2) ⅜″ × ⅜″ × 18″ walnut
Side mouldings (2) ⅜″ × ⅜″ × 11″ walnut

Decorative Box

MASON RAPAPORT

NAME: Mason Rapaport
HOME: Easthampton, Massachusetts
PROJECT: Decorative Box
DIMENSIONS: 3″ × 4″ × 7″
MATERIALS: Walnut
FINISH: Watco, polyurethane
TIME SPENT: 2 days
MATERIALS COST: scrap

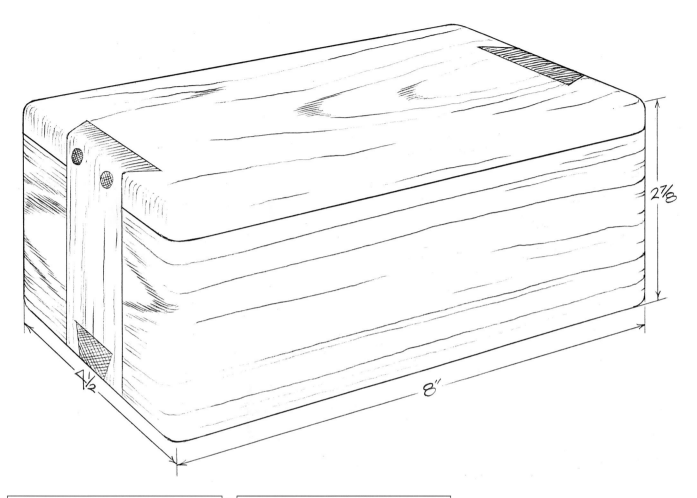

Professional furniture maker, though originally educated in finance, Mason Rapaport apprenticed with Roger Heitzman Woodworking for six months in 1990. For the past few years he has been busy creating his own designs and showing them in exhibitions around the country. When asked about the inspiration for the boxes in this book, which were gifts to friends, he replied, "I wanted to build boxes that would be simple to build as well as fun and nice to look at."

PROJECT DESCRIPTION

Basically this is a band sawn box. The end latches are held in place by a sliding dovetail that runs along the bottom of the box.

Lidded Box
MASON RAPAPORT

NAME: Mason Rapaport
HOME: Easthampton, Massachusetts
PROJECT: Lidded Box
DIMENSIONS: 10″ × 4″ × 2¾″
MATERIALS: Cherry, walnut
FINISH: Watco, polyurethane
TIME SPENT: 2 days
MATERIALS COST: scrap

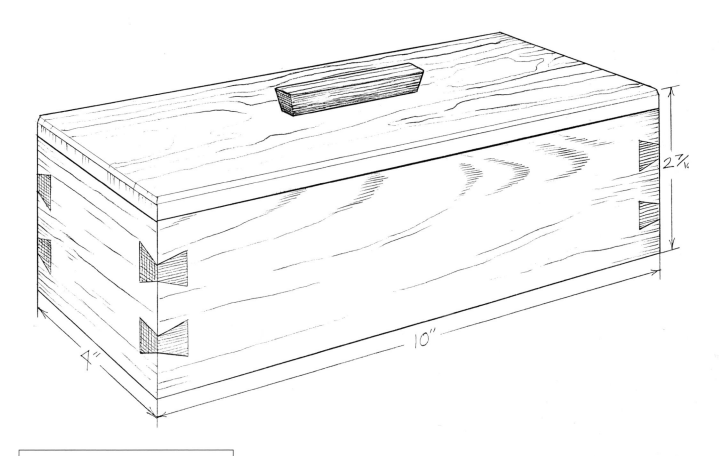

2 7/16

10"

4"

PROJECT DESCRIPTION

Most of the joints for this box are mitered corners held together with dovetailed splines. The top of the box sides are rabbetted to form a recess into which the bottom of the lid fits. The bottom is captured in dadoes in the sides of the box.

Vigas
SEATON WOOD DESIGN

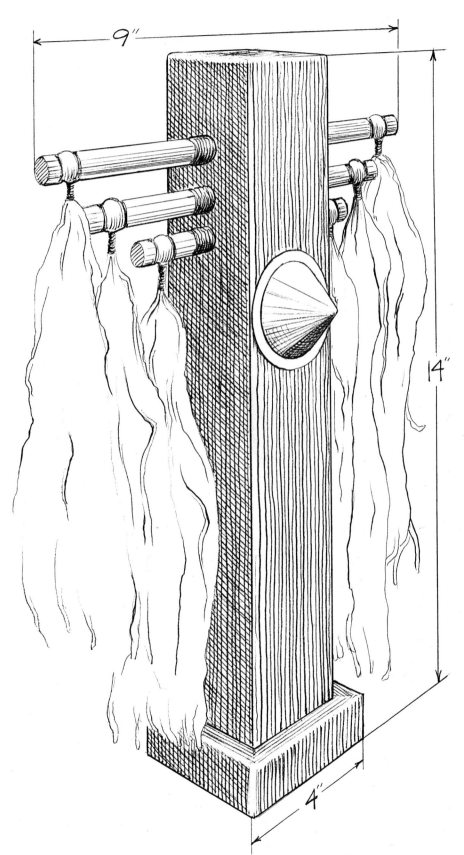

9″

14″

4″

J EFFREY SEATON has become prominently known nationally, as well as internationally, for his devotion to quality combined with imagination that are reflected in his one-of-a-kind containers. His work is currently on display at the New York Museum of Modern Art as part of their permanent collection. When asked about the inspiration for this box, he explained, "While traveling in New Mexico, we were influenced by the local architecture and native American influences. The poles used for roofing that extend beyond the walls of adobe houses are called 'vigas,' hence the title 'Vigas.'"

PROJECT DESCRIPTION

The turned Brazilwood knob pierces the front of the ebony container and enters the "inner lid," thus locking the top in place. Gold leaf is used on a brass disc to add contrast and more color. Raffia (a natural fiber) is split and dyed to add color and texture.

NAME: Seaton Wood Design (Jeffrey and Katrina Seaton)
HOME: Ojai, California
PROJECT: Vigas
DIMENSIONS: 14″ × 9″ × 3″
MATERIALS: Ebony, Brazilwood
FINISH: Livos natural oils, carnauba wax
TIME SPENT: 4-6 hours
MATERIALS COST: $50
RETAIL PRICE: $1,000

Ebony Wing

SEATON WOOD DESIGN

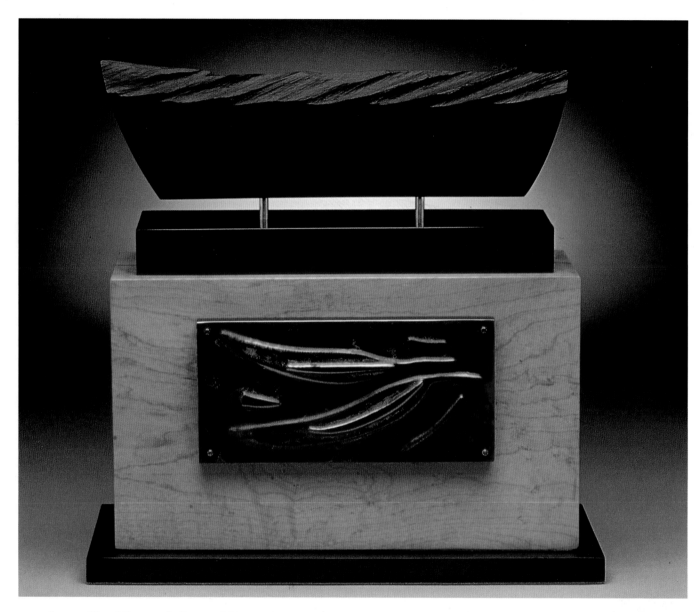

NAME: Seaton Wood Design (Jeffrey and Katrina Seaton)

HOME: Ojai, California

PROJECT: Ebony Wing

DIMENSIONS: 12″ × 12″ × 6″

MATERIALS: Ebony, bird's-eye maple

FINISH: Oil, wax

TIME SPENT: 6-8 hours

MATERIALS COST: $50

RETAIL PRICE: $900

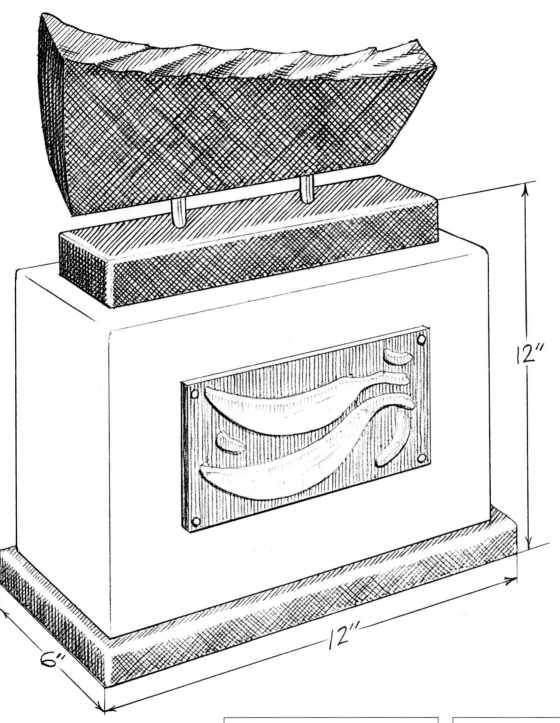

12"

12"

6"

T his box is purely for ornamental
    purposes. The boat/ark is the
"flowing of nature" combined with
highly polished surfaces. The contrast between the textured top of
the handle, of black and white, balance out an aesthetically appealing
form.

PROJECT DESCRIPTION

Two 8/4 maple boards are laminated
for width. Sterling silver tubes are
used to float the wing handle over the
box lid.